GROWING IN FRIENDSHIP WITH GOD

DISCOVERING THE *Joy* OF *Lent*

CYCLE C
YEAR 2019

Fr. Andrew Carl Wisdom, O.P.
and Dominican Friars,
Province of St. Albert the Great

Other Publications by Fr. Wisdom, O.P.:

Preaching to a Multigenerational Assembly (Liturgical Press, 2004)
Advent and Christmas Wisdom from St. Thomas Aquinas (Liguori, 2009)
Tuning In to God's Call (Liguori, 2012)
The Official Study Guide: Tuning In to God's Call (New Priory Press, 2016)
Family, the Church, and the Real World - contributing author (Liguori, 2015)
Make of Your Life a Gift: Letters of Gratitude (New Priory Press, 2016)
Growing in Friendship with God: Cycle B (New Priory Press, 2018)
"Why Should I Encourage My Son to Be a Priest?" (Liguori, 2007)

Published by New Priory Press
1910 South Ashland Avenue
Chicago, IL 60608

www.NewPrioryPress.com

© New Priory Press 2019

Edited by: Bob Dixon
Production Editor: Terry L. Jarbe

Printed and bound in the United States of America

NEW PRIORY PRESS
EXPLORING THE DOMINICAN VISION

Dedication

To our deceased fellow Dominican Friars now fully embraced in friendship with God. Their memory continues to inspire our growth as St. Dominic's sons.

Province of St. Albert the Great

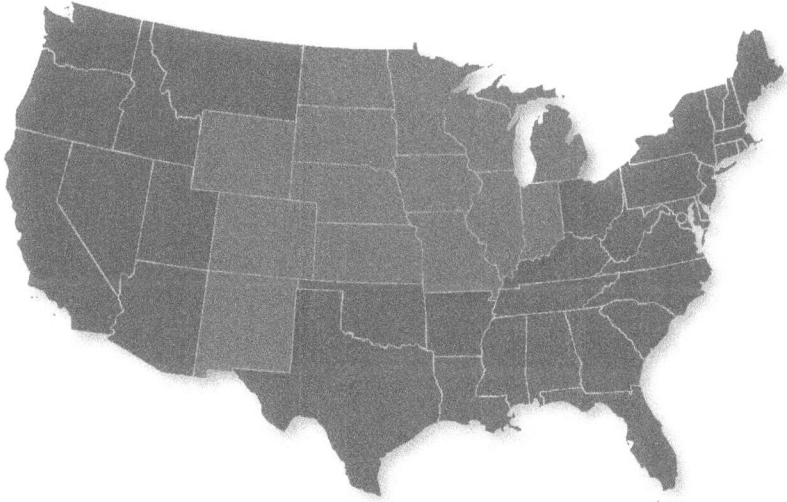

Parishes

Blessed Sacrament • Madison, WI

Holy Rosary/Santo Rosario •
  Minneapolis, MN

St. Albert the Great • Minneapolis, MN

St. Dominic • Denver, CO

St. Pius V • Chicago, IL

St. Vincent Ferrer • River Forest, IL

Campus Ministry

St. Paul Catholic Center •
  Indiana University

St. Thomas Aquinas Newman Center •
  Purdue University

St. Thomas More Newman Center •
  University of Missouri-Columbia

Education/Spirituality

Aquinas Institute of Theology •
  St. Louis, MO

Dominican Ecclesial Institute •
  Albuquerque, NM

Fenwick High School • Oak Park, IL

Shrine of St. Jude • Chicago, IL

Contents

Foreword

Dear Friend:

Welcome to the joyful season of Lent. It is not always referred to as "joyful," yet, mysteriously and profoundly so, JOYFUL IT IS! Members of the Order of Preachers, and especially those of us who work daily in this holy charism of preaching, wish to share some spiritual gifts with all who remain a part of our life and ministry year round.

Inspired by our founder, St. Dominic, and the challenge he presented to his budding band of preachers, St. Thomas Aquinas wrote in his famous *Summa Theologiae*, "Contemplate, and share the fruits of your contemplation with others" (*contemplata aliis tradere*). These words, at the very heart of the Sacred Preaching, compel all Dominicans to reflect on the Word of God and to share the fruits of that reflection with whomever we encounter. The scriptures, alive and well in the world today, remain a source of inspiration, grace, and hope to all who embrace them. We Dominicans wish to serve as humble agents of that encounter with God's Word.

Each day during the season of Lent, a friar of the Province of St. Albert the Great provides a short reflection on the liturgical readings of the day, and Fr. Wisdom offers his prayerful contemplation, calls to action and helpful hints. We pray these words will be a source of renewed faith and deepened hope as we journey with the Lord during these 40 days of Lent. May they lead us all to an exultant Easter celebration of the Resurrection of Jesus Christ.

I pray that the fruits of these friar contemplations may inspire within you a deep confidence in God's all-abiding love for us. In turn, may these reflections serve to welcome you more closely into the lives of the Dominican Friars who minister in the central United States and many other parts of the world.

Blessings for a deeply holy Lenten Season,

Very Reverend James V. Marchionda, OP
Prior Provincial, Province of St. Albert the Great

Prayer Fasting Almsgiving

Preface

"Lent is a new beginning, a path leading to the certain goal of Easter, Christ's victory over death. This season urgently calls us to conversion. Christians are asked to return to God 'with all their hearts' (Joel 2:12), to refuse to settle for mediocrity and to grow in friendship with the Lord. Jesus is the faithful friend who never abandons us. Even when we sin, he patiently awaits our return; by that patient expectation, he shows us his readiness to forgive (cf. Homily, 8 January 2016)."

Pope Francis

My friends, family and fellow Dominican friars know me as "a saver." Nevertheless, they have encouraged me in recent years as I throw away more and more of my "treasured possessions." As I conscientiously tackled a cabinet in my office in December 2017, I came across a saved collection of Lenten reflections prayerfully conceived by my brothers for publication on our Province website (opcentral.org) several years ago. We wanted these reflections to serve as a form of daily prayer and preaching for our many friends and benefactors of the Order. An ancient motto of the Order is "to be useful to the souls of others." This provided a very modern way to do just that.

At the risk of cliché, this has been a labor of love. Reading through and mediating on my brothers' reflections, I was touched by the enduring spiritual depth, insight, academic scholarship and daily practicality of my brothers, old and young, living and deceased. Prayerful conversation with the Lord naturally flowed out. I took the liberty of adding the fruit of my prayer to each daily reflection. Following each prayer, I've included practical suggestions to aid the conversion Pope Francis reminds us that we are called to in this season.

Christian faith is a "contact sport," after all. It doesn't happen sitting in the stands, but while actively engaged on the field. Therefore, I've also added my own imperatives in a section dubbed, *Doer of the Word Received*, taken from St. James' entreaty, "Be doers of the Word, and not just hearers only, deluding yourselves" (James 1:22). Additional space is provided in a *Notes* section to help you complete your homework on time. No excuses!

Moments like these find me profoundly grateful for my vocation as a member of the Order of Preachers. In these reflections, my brothers continue to teach me how to become a better Christian and faithful son of St. Dominic. I am especially excited to include the words of my fellow friars who have finished their Christian pilgrimage on this earth. Through their words, they speak to us even as they enjoy the eternal light promised to us at Easter and testify to the Gospel's enduring transcendence. What our brothers once preached on earth, they now experience eternally in heaven. May it be so for us all!

Fr. Andrew Carl Wisdom, O.P.
Dominican Province of St. Albert the Great

GROWING IN FRIENDSHIP WITH GOD

DISCOVERING THE *Joy* OF *Lent*

Ash Wednesday

JL 2:12-18; MT 6:1-6, 16-18

"Even now, says the Lord, return to me with all of your heart." As we begin this joyful season of Lent, we hear the concerned, compassionate voice of a loving parent calling us home. Even after all we have done or not done, we are wanted with an intensity of love that is beyond merciful measure. The call, however, is not for tomorrow, but today! We realize how precious and urgent today is when we receive ashes. We are reminded that we are dust and to dust we shall return. What we are to do with today is to return it, dust particles and all, to the gracious hands who gave it to us by rending "our hearts not our garments." The heart is the seat of our motivations. When I give alms to the materially or emotionally poor, do I do it for God's glory or mine? When I pray, is it for God's praise or mine? When I fast from food or foul judgments, do I do it to point to God or to myself? All of human history is but a love affair between Creator and creature. In Lent, we hit the liturgical pause button to be reminded that our most important relationship is ultimately an affair of the heart. That Divine Heart creates my human heart anew.

Fr. Andrew Carl Wisdom, O.P.
Professed: 1999
Vicar for Mission Advancement and
Director of the Society for Vocational Support
Chicago, IL

Heavenly Father:

As we begin this sacred season of Lent, help us to recognize while we are made of dust and will return to dust, we are much more than mere dust in your eyes, for you have made us little less than angels. We cannot begin to imagine just how much you love us, treasure us and delight in our company! If we did, we would not be so slow to return to you with all our hearts. We would not have wandered away in the first place, drifting from this attraction to that attraction only to find them all distractions from what our hearts truly yearn for: your love. Help us to begin Lent well. First, by recognizing we are looking for love and approval and healing in all the wrong places. Second by realizing you are the ultimate love our hearts seek and you are enough! In truth, yours is the only voice we want to hear calling us back home to your heart. For only you can fill our heart's deepest longing.

Doer of the Word Received: I will take a mini-inventory of my life today and identify two or three clear issues holding me back from making a full return of my heart to God, my true longing. *HINT: Start with common everyday attractions that have become distractions.*

Notes:

Thursday after Ash Wednesday

DT 30: 15-20; LK 9: 22-25

We have said in a prayer on Ash Wednesday the following words, "Lord, Bless these ashes by which we show that we are dust. Pardon our sins and keep us faithful to the discipline of Lent. For you do not want sinners to die but to live with the risen Christ." We are dust and we shall return to dust one day. Remain in me not for a few hours, but remain in me for my whole preparation for eternal life. Our life shall be a preparation for the coming of the Lord in our lives. We shall recollect that Christ gave himself to dying for us, to giving himself wholly, of body and soul for us. We shall all be changed into his love for us. If we shall be like Christ in our personal life, we must put aside various vices, such as, anger, envy, all resentments that we may have, spiritual laziness, illicit desires that are in the soul. We shall put aside any darkness that is in the soul and we shall clothe ourselves with the light of the virtues that we need. We shall begin to clothe ourselves with the various virtues. We shall see God's will in everything that we do. We shall begin to love God in what we do, trying to love our neighbor in all we do. Let your light shine before men that they may glorify your Heavenly Father and reign forever in Heaven. (I give credit for these ideas to Blessed Elizabeth of the Trinity, a French Carmelite nun. She died in 1906.)

Fr. Raphael Fabish, O.P.
Professed: 1947
Limited service
Chicago, IL

Tender God:

Teach us the discipline of love this Lent. True love is not a fair-weather friend that only shows up when things are well, but a disciplined friend constant in loving no matter the circumstances of day or night; whether the sun is shining or the clouds are raining. All true disciples, like all great athletes, adhere to a very special discipline; one that carries us through the good and the bad, the positive and the negative, the cross and the crown. It is this discipline of love that counts the cost only at the beginning of the journey, and then commits once the adventure into the terrain of your Divine Heart is launched. Loving you demands no less than our full commitment.

Doer of the Word Received: Reflect upon the honest level of your commitment to being a daily disciple of Jesus Christ. Are you constant and consistent? *HINT: If discipline is lacking in other areas of your life, it will have a direct effect on the discipline of your spiritual commitment, for example, your prayer life.*

Notes:

Friday after Ash Wednesday

IS 58:1-9A; MT 9: 14-15

The expression 'festive fasting' is an oxymoron: "a rhetorical figure in which incongruous or contradictory terms are combined." There can be little that is festive about fasting from food or eating very little. But it can have a festive flavor.

In the gospel reading, the disciples of John approach Jesus and ask why they fast, but his own do not. He responds that the reason they don't do so is that the bridegroom, Jesus himself, is still with them. But the day is coming when they will fast. Jesus says in chapter 6 of Matthew's gospel account: "When you fast do not look gloomy like the hypocrites ... But when you fast, anoint your head and wash your face ..."

The Gospel has been called 'a rehearsal of our table manners.' It requires learning how to behave properly, how to live in accord with the teachings and example of Jesus, who warned against looking gloomy like the hypocrites when fasting.

Lenten fasting can be joyous because of the anticipated festive celebration of the Lord's resurrection. It prepares us for taking our place, with anointed head and cleansed face, at the eternal banquet in God's Kingdom.

Fr. Joseph Fogarty, O.P.
Professed: 1953
Entered Into Eternal Life: January 26, 2016

Dearest Jesus:
A spiritually festive joy is your calling card; the overwhelming evidence that convicts us as your disciples. You call us to this authentic joy through fasting. You call us in todays' reading, this Lent, to be filled up by emptying ourselves. Give us the courage to go counter to the cultural compulsion to fill ourselves by accumulating more rather than living with less; less judgement, less gossip, less envy, less comparison, less competitiveness. Help us let go of possessions, projects and even people we have only gathered for our own benefit. Fasting from these lesser things, may we taste more fully of you!

Doer of the Word Received: What are you overindulging in to excess in your life right now? What have you accumulated that God is saying you don't need and asking you to let go of this Lent? *HINT: Start by looking at what you have stored in overstuffed closets.*

Notes:

Saturday after Ash Wednesday

IS 58:9B-14; LK 5:27-32

Try Less for Lent! How's that for a Lenten thought? But I'm serious. I think that too often, in trying to respond to Jesus' call, "Follow me," people try to do too much too fast, especially in a season like Lent. For example, deciding to attend daily Mass as your Lenten practice and then, when it becomes "just too hard," just giving up and ending up doing nothing. I'd like to suggest moderation. For example, just say ten Hail Marys for deceased relatives every day. Another thought, while you're waiting in line at the supermarket or for the bus, start praying for deceased loved ones. It makes the wait seem shorter and is certainly more productive. Coaches have athletes start out at a lower level of exercise and then gradually build up to the more strenuous. Maybe we can learn a spiritual lesson from them! Start out small. . . and then gradually increase our penance and prayers. See you at Easter!

Fr. Walter O'Connell, O.P.
Professed: 1951
Limited service
Chicago, IL

Holy Spirit of God:
Please be my guide and coach this Lent. I know I'm not the easiest person to work with, so settled in my ways of thinking, acting and speaking. This Lent, I really want to give myself over to your compassionate direction; your program for spiritual growth, not mine. I so want to relinquish control of my life into your hands. I so want to give up the illusion I am running things, I am in charge. Then I can pray more honestly and credibly that prayer I pray too often with too little honesty or credibility: "YOUR kingdom come, YOUR will be done." In other words, "My kingdom go, my will let go."

Doer of the Word Received: Honestly examine your control issues. In what situations are you "willful?" What is it costing you in the way of lack of peace, continual anxiety and endless worry? Where is God inviting you to let go? *HINT: Where do YOU always have to be in charge? Briefly list recent situations you felt stole your peace, caused you anxiety, or gave you worry.*

Notes:

First Sunday of Lent

DT 26:4-10; 1 ROM 10:8-13; LK 4:1-13

Our Gospel story is not simply about "what" choices (about bread, power or who Jesus worships). It is rather the story of how Jesus decides who he would be as an adult. He had no choice about what: He is the Son of God! But how would He be this Son of God? This is a story of Jesus' struggle, of his doubts and questioning which the evangelist calls temptation. Like us, Jesus was confronted with a crucial decision: either choose to use his power in isolation on his own behalf, or to use his power to find his own identity with and for others. Jesus was tempted to make bread for himself, to gain personal power and control, and to worship a lesser (perhaps more immediately satisfying) God.

Like Jesus, the temptation we all face in seeking to become more fully human is to use our power for short-term personal goals only. To choose anything that does not promote your good as well as mine, is to choose for myself at your expense. When we choose short-term personal rewards at the expense of others, we both lose. When I oppress you today, we both lose our freedom tomorrow. When I gossip or spread rumors to make me feel superior to someone, we are all affected. When I grow rich at your expense today, we will both be poor tomorrow. What we believe as Catholic Christians is that what affects you affects me. We need one another to find our authentic identity and destiny. We are one body. We are one family.

Fr. Jim Spahn, O.P.
Professed: 1977
Pastor
St. Dominic Parish
Denver, CO

Beloved Son of God:

You really were like us in all things but sin when you walked this earth! Help me better grasp that reality that I may more fully appreciate that you really do know what I am going through. You really do know what it is to be assaulted with doubts, temptations, and trials from out of nowhere. You are no stranger to anxiety, fear and confusion. Son of God, strengthen this adopted brother, this adopted daughter with the solace of this truth so that in my insecure moments I don't gossip or oppress others in an effort to be superior. You walked our steps first. You know firsthand, sorrow and pain, disappointment and regret. You are intimate with rejection and mockery and misunderstanding. You also know intense joy in your faith in your heavenly Father, the peace of integrity in a clear life, purpose, and immense happiness in the company of your family, friends and fellow Kingdom-builders. In these graced realities, help me to find my authentic identity and destiny as you did.

Doer of the Word Received: Take a few minutes in the middle of your day to stop and reflect on whether you are living out your long-term authentic identity and destiny as the intimate friend and disciple of Jesus Christ. Examine your conscience. Are there short-term, self-centered goals in the way that run roughshod over others at home or work? Close your eyes now and put your head on His shoulder or across His breast as the beloved disciple did and have a candid, direct talk with the Lord. Feel His heart beating as He takes one breath after another and know it beats for you! And say simply, "Lord, thank you for being here with me. Show me my actual attitudes and actions in this moment and help me to change what is not worthy of a friend of yours." *HINT: Review your recent interactions and imagine if Christ were standing right there with you aware of their sincerity and intent. Jot down on a small piece of paper what you resolve to change and only throw it out when it does!*

Notes:

Monday of the First Week of Lent

LV 19:1-2, 11-18; MT 25:31-46

The readings for today raise many troubling questions for us about what is expected of the followers of Jesus Christ, how well we Christians live what we believe. Often we may find ourselves struggling with the question of what is the right thing to do in this particular situation, what should I say or what action is called for in this set of circumstances. It may be deciding what is most important to consider as I try to resolve what I am to do. Sometimes it involves dealing with the distinction between what the letter of the law demands, as the reading from the book of Leviticus states, and what the spirit of the law seems to call into play as a balance to a legalistic approach to life. The passage from the Gospel of Matthew reminds us of the significance of that spiritual attitude spelled out in the works of mercy that Jesus uses as examples for how we should be attentive to our sisters and brothers in need. And, there is the further implication that in God's way of justice we really end up making a judgment on ourselves by what we do or fail to do. It is the fruit of our good works, our considered decisions and our overall approach to living in the spirit of Jesus by which we will be judged, and that judgment is a result of what we have freely chosen. Those who are faithful followers of Jesus in extending God's way of life are called to evaluate their own thoughts, words and actions in light of Gospel values.

The bottom line for those who want to live rightly, with a healthy balance between law and spirit, is that central rule from Jesus' teaching: treat others as you would like to be treated whether your neighbor is a friend or someone you do not like. Can Lent be a time when we allow our spirit to rest peacefully with God's spirit so that we can engage in an honest self-evaluation and thus, in the future, more truly reflect a genuineness of care for our brothers and sisters?

Fr. Harry Byrne, O.P.
Professed: 1974
Professor Emeritus
Aquinas Institute of Theology
St. Louis, MO

Sacred Teacher:

Fill me with your Spirit that I may be true to what I profess to believe. Give me the courage to see myself as I truly am this Lent. Help me to see in "the other" I encounter, whether I like them or not, your face staring back at me. Break down my hardened heart and give me a heart softened by this Lent. Help me examine my thoughts, words and deeds in light of the gospel values you gave us that I might fulfill not just the letter of the law, but its spirit. Resting peacefully in your Spirit, may I discover a greater freedom to see beyond my own wants to the genuine needs of my brothers and sisters around me each day.

Doer of the Word Received: Examine your thoughts, words and deeds in the last 24 hours. Have they been true to what you profess to believe? *HINT: Was I interiorly disturbed and lacking peace after something I thought, said, or did in the last 24 hours?*

Notes:

Tuesday of the First Week of Lent

IS 55:10-11, MT 6:7-15

In this Lenten season of repentance, we can get so caught up in the greatness of our sin that we forget what is truly great: God's unwearied love and mercy. No matter how far we run from the Lord, His promise remains: "My love shall never leave you nor my covenant of peace be shaken" (Isaiah 54:10). Ultimately, Christ's mission on Earth is to reconcile humanity to God. It is with that objective that He teaches us in today's Gospel to pray "Our Father... forgive us our debts, as we forgive our debtors." But oh, how we can cling to our sinfulness and refuse to be forgiven! We deem ourselves unworthy of God's love and mercy, setting up barriers to a loving Father who knows all we have done and is longing to embrace us just the same. We deem ourselves unforgivable and thus ignore the promise God gives us through His prophet Isaiah today: Christ has come forth from God not to "return to [the Father] void," but to "do [His] will, achieving the end for which" He was sent. This end was reconciliation. It was accomplished once and for all on the wood of the Cross that Lent leads us to. This season of Lent, do not devoid the Cross of its power. Allow God to forgive you and stop running from His embrace.

Fr. Vincent Dávila, O.P.
Professed: 2011
Faculty Member and Campus Minister
University of St. Thomas
St. Paul, MN

God of Unwearied Love and Mercy:
You did not send your Son to condemn us, but to save us. You stretch out your hand to lift us up from the darkness of our sinful self-absorption into the light of your face. In gazing on you and not myself, may I know what it is to be forgiven…and forgive others their sins, including myself. May I at long last stop running from your embrace, but run eagerly toward it…and lose myself in it!

Doer of the Word Received: Ask for forgiveness today for something you have done wrong no matter how small. *HINT: What have I done that still bothers my conscience even if it seems trivial?*

Notes:

Wednesday of the First Week of Lent

JON 3:1-10; LK 11:29-32

So often when we read or hear about the prophet Jonah, the first image we form is that of a man swallowed by a whale, but who is eventually discharged from the whale's interior darkness. We know that this story is a prefigurement and a prophecy of Jesus' death and burial in the tomb, and then his resurrection. But when Jesus says that no sign will be given to an evil generation except the sign of Jonah, he is referring to Jonah as a fearless preacher who foreshadows Jesus' own preaching.

Indeed, Jesus' preaching in today's Gospel is not only fearless, but also fierce and passionate. He calls the present generation evil, worthy of harsh judgment. It is to be condemned absolutely.

As I meditate on Jesus' words, do I hear them addressing me personally? This season of Lent reminds me that there is always a time for repentance in my life. I am always being called to become my better self. There is a yearning in my heart for becoming a person of integrity. But this call cannot be adequately responded to unless there is repentance in my life. I must acknowledge my moral failures, reject them and replace them with positive acts of love and justice.

Fr. Richard LaPata, O.P.
Professed: 1953
Limited Service
River Forest, IL

Dearest Jesus:

I can be so filled with fear...of my own unworthiness, my failures and, in truth, even of my own goodness. I can be so fearful of the rejection I may receive when I stand up for your gospel of life and love and light. Give me the fearless courage of your prophet, Jonah, if just for a moment...that moment when it can really make a difference. Help me realize I am not merely called to preach your gospel with words, but by the very way I live my life. Can others see how you live in me? Will they be moved to likewise open their hearts and minds to you? Make me your fearless preacher, not pretending perfection, but accepting of my own imperfection and therefore free to love others in their imperfection as well.

Doer of the Word Received: Before going to bed tonight, stand up for the yospel of life, love and light though a conversation face to face, via phone or through a note. *HINT: Whom have you recently regretted not confronting lovingly when a challenge was needed?*

Notes:

Thursday of the First Week of Lent

EST C:12, 14-16, 23-25; MT 7:7-12

"Inquiring minds want to know." This was a familiar advertising tagline from a popular tabloid years ago many will remember. Of course, to know or get the information desired, one must ask or seek. It is in the asking or seeking we receive. This simple task is different for us as Christians, for we ask and seek in faith.

Lent is a journey of faith where we continue to ask, seek and knock, as Jesus in the Gospel for today directs us. We ask ourselves a few questions: "For whom or what are we asking or seeking, and on what or whose door are we knocking?" The answer is quite simple. We seek God. We seek God to grow in a deeper relationship with Him and we ask for greater insight and help in difficult times in life, such as illness, family and relationship difficulties, faith questions, spiritual growth, direction, and many other questions of our day. We live in a rapidly changing world. The world of technology can both help and hinder our spiritual journey. It can be confusing to know and seek the truth. Yet we seek God, for we know God is the fullness of truth and love.

God longs for our engagement and waits patiently for us as we ask, seek and knock. We all inquire in a unique way. Some ask or speak directly to God, some seek, or look for God all around them, and others knock or go out and find God in the world of their life and vocation. No matter how we "inquire," God will always hear us and give us what we need, not always what we want.

As we travel the journey of Lent in the midst of our daily routine, we remember our desire is to know, to love and to live the heart of Jesus!

Fr. Louis Morrone, O.P.
Professed: 1987
Socius & Vicar Provincial
Province of St. Albert the Great
Chicago, IL

18

God, the Fulfillment of All Desire:
Help me to desire you alone. Teach me how to ask and seek in faith. Give me the courage to knock repeatedly on the door of your heart. I know that is the road to you, but sometimes I just don't know how to talk to you. I wonder if my need or want is too little or silly to bother you with. Surely you have bigger things to deal with. Sometimes, I just feel too ashamed to approach you, painfully mindful of past sins and present distractions. Sometimes, the silence is so deafening from this end I wonder if you are even there. Yet, in faith, I know you cannot but hear every prayer uttered your direction. Even a sincere glance of my heart your way I know in faith touches your heart.

Renew in me this Lent that graced certainty that inspires the courage to ask for what I need and want; to seek your will in all things no matter where it leads me. Help me to knock on the door of your heart each day and know in my heart that, while you will not always give me what I want, you will always give me what I need.

Doer of the Word Received: Take a walk today with God. Knock on the door of His heart. Pound if you must! Say, "Lord, it's me! I just want you to know it is you I seek in this situation, in this person, in this task before me. I ask for your guidance in this moment and I trust in faith you will be here whether I feel it or not. I love you, Lord!" *HINT: We have time to take a 10 or 15 minute walk, wherever we are, home or work. It is not the length of the walk with God, but the quality of the talk with God.*

Notes:

Friday of the First Week of Lent

EZ 18: 21-28, MT 5: 20-26

Today we hear the first of six short paragraphs. Taken together the six paragraphs are the ethical heart of the Sermon on the Mount. They remain, even after two thousand years, a challenge for healthy people to live out. Together they form a part of the greater righteousness or justice of which Jesus speaks in the first verse (v. 20). Today we are dealing with a serious matter, a murder. You shall not kill. Jesus applies this commandment, which deals with extreme cases, to everyday life. We are not tempted to murder every day, but we may be tempted to anger often enough. Jesus speaks of anger and of an escalation of insults: anger, empty-head, fool!

He implies: we can kill with words, with emotions, also with lack of emotion, indifference, coldness. This is shown in the two added examples. Fraternal harmony and reconciliation take precedence even over worship. "The anger of man worketh not the righteousness of God" (James 1 :20). But this teaching against anger has another side to it. In the Old Testament God is often portrayed as angry with the Israelites because of their faithlessness. God praises the priest Phinehas for his zeal and for his anger (Numbers 25). Jesus himself drives the money-changers out of the Temple, and, according to John, with a whip (John 2:13-22).

Psychologists tell us that much mental illness is caused by repressed anger. Anger is therefore an important part of our emotional life. We must treasure our anger and learn how to harness its energy. We should also try to find positive ways to express our anger, whether in work or in sport or in piano-playing. We should not deny our anger or repress it. We should recognize it, at least to ourselves. Then we have a better chance to control it and to use it for good. On the basis of psychological honesty, we can build a sincere fraternity.

Fr. Benedict Thomas Viviano, O.P.
Professed: 1960
Professor Emeritus
University of Fribourg
Vienna, Austria

Spirit of God:

Infuse me with your love and light, especially when I am prone to anger. Help me to see my brother and sister as you see them, that I may love them as you love them and that my anger may cool in the light of love. Teach me how to love even during conflict and to sincerely seek reconciliation and harmony with those with whom I persistently struggle. Authentic virtue is born amid the many invitations to vice. Where I would be envious, help me relinquish the temptation to shallow comparison. Where I would be judgmental, help me be grateful for the gift of "the other." Where I would be angry, help me speak a candor inviting peaceful resolution. While not denying or repressing my anger, help it not to consume me and the person before me you call, "Beloved Son, Beloved Daughter."

Doer of the Word Received: Identify someone you have been envious of, judgmental toward or angry with. Address the situation on your own or with help. _HINT: Start with the first person that comes to mind as you pray this reflection._

Notes:

Saturday of the First Week of Lent

DT 26:16-19; MT 5:43-48

One of the most wonderful discoveries we can make on our Lenten journey is a better understanding of who God really is. Our readings highlight just how wonderful and important a gift Jesus' birth and life with us are and were. Without the understanding we gained by having the gift of God living among us, our two readings today may lead us to think that God changed His mind somewhere between the time of Moses, when the covenant we read about in the book of Deuteronomy, and what Jesus is telling people about during the Sermon on the Mount, which is where our Gospel reading is situated. When Jesus says, "You have heard it said… but I say to you…," he is not challenging the "law" or the "rules" laid out by God through Moses. He is challenging what people thought the law and the teaching of the prophets meant. Popular opinion both in the religious sense and cultural sense had drifted quite far from the true teaching of God.

One of the gifts we prepare for during Lent and then celebrate and remember at Easter, is the fact that God Himself, in the person of Jesus, came not only to tell us but to show us through examples like we find in today's Gospel, what God's love is truly like. Jesus is telling us that we need to reach out in love to those whom do not seem to love us. Jesus is, in essence, saying, "God even loves those who do not seem to love Him."

How often does popular culture tell us we should not love those who are different or disagree with our own personal views and beliefs? How often in your life have you "heard it said…" only to hear the Gospel respond, "Amen. Amen. But I say to you…?" The great gift is in following the Gospel. That way we never go astray!

Fr. Michail Ford, O.P.
Professed: 2004
Parochial Vicar
St. Vincent Ferrer Parish
River Forest, IL

Generous God:
You not only tell us, but show us in the most profound way what your love looks like: you give us your own beloved son. Through the person of Jesus, we no longer wonder what you are like, whether or not you love us or what you ask of us. It is all there in His example. It is all there in His words. It is all there in His preaching, healing, and praying. Do we hear the voice of Jesus? Are we listening for its direction? How often have we "heard it said" about some issue in contemporary culture, but not listened to your Son, Jesus, whispering within, "But I say to you" the truth about the very same topic? Give us generous ears today, God of generosity, that we might hear anew your message though Jesus to be patient with those who don't seem to love us, to be patient with those who don't love you. Rather, may our witness of generosity be so great, even as we defend the truths of the gospel, that they know we are Christians by our love; that they know without a doubt we belong to you.

Doer of the Word Received: Examine your thinking about the teachings of God you have encountered in this first week of Lent. Recall where you have drifted in approaching material goods or charity to the less fortunate or sexuality or attendance at Sunday Eucharist, not as Christ has taught but rather as our culture now seems to demand. Talk to a fellow Christian today about where you may have blurred the lines and become a "cultural Christian" on these issues, thinking like everyone else. *HINT: Have that talk with someone who challenges you and doesn't allow you to play small in your life. The answer to the question above lies in where you are not actively living your faith, but merely coasting along in it.*

Notes:

Second Sunday of Lent

GN 15:5-12, 17-18; PHIL 3:17-4:1; LK 9:28B-36

St. Mother Teresa of Calcutta said that one day a young sister came in the door and her face was shining with joy. St. Mother Teresa asked her what she had been doing. She said that for the last two hours, she had been touching Jesus. She had been lovingly picking maggots off a man who was lying by the side of the road.

By faith, this young sister saw Jesus in this man who was dying alone by the side of the road. She took very literally the words of Jesus, "Whatever you do to the least of my brothers, you do unto me."

And how do you think the man felt? Before she came, he was dying alone by the side of the road, and now someone was treating him as if he were God Himself. Before, he felt like a nobody. Now, he knew he was somebody. Before, he felt abandoned and rejected; now, he knew he was loved and precious. Before, he was like an abandoned orphan. Now he knew he was a beloved child of God.

When we treat others with great love, we will catch a glimpse of the glory of the Lord in them, and they, themselves, will become aware of their own goodness and beauty.

I think that both the sister and the man had a transfiguration experience. By faith, the sister saw the glory of Jesus in the man, and she watched as the glory of the Lord shone forth in the man, and they both became aware of God's glory in themselves and in one another. Perhaps they said to themselves, 'Lord, it is good for us to be here.'

Fr. Ed Riley, O.P.
Professed: 1954
Limited Service
Chicago, IL

Jesus of Many Disguises:
Stop me in my often-mindless tracks and draw me into your presence all around me. Confront my indifference in the eyes of those who stand before me disguised as you. Touch my distracted heart in the heart of the other standing in front of me, masked as someone separate from me, but in truth my brother or sister in you. Recognizing you in them, challenge me to risk the inconvenience of getting involved, the fear of getting my hands dirty in loving them and the belief that says they are someone else's problem. Only then Jesus, will I be transfigured into your glory. Only then will I have the irrational, uncommon sense, but faith-sense to not run away from you in my brother and sister before me. Compel me to joyfully proclaim, "It is good that we are here!"

Doer of the Word Received: Each day offers countless examples for the Christian disciple transfigured in Christ to stop and engage those in need around him or her; those impoverished not just materially, but emotionally, psychologically or spiritually. Suspend part of your agenda and to-do list for today to help another. Remember, God loves a cheerful giver! *HINT: It could be that person we probably like the least or a familiar stranger among us who is nagging us, that face haunting us in the back of our head right now who we are avoiding. Decide today how you will approach him or her as if approaching Christ Himself.*

Notes:

Monday of the Second Week of Lent

DN 9:4B-10; LK 6:36-38

What is it that we "measure out" to others, and what does God measure out to us? The Prophet Daniel today says that what the people have measured out to each other is not according to God's commandments, and so they have the measure of shame and guilt. But that measure does not compare with God's measure of "compassion and forgiveness". Jesus gives us the same thing to measure out: "Be merciful, just as your Father is merciful." We are not to measure out judgment. Lent does not mean that we burden ourselves—life offers enough burdens—and the desert fathers said, "Judging others is a heavy burden." As Henri Nouwen has said, if we can free ourselves from the need and the heavy burden of judging others, we don't mind carrying the light burden of being judged by God.

Fr. John Risley, O.P.
Professed: 1959
Chaplain
Dominican Motherhouse
Sinsinawa, WI

Merciful Father:

You are so patient with me and my faults and sins. Why can't I be just as patient with the faults of others? Lord, before I know it, all someone must do is walk into a room or come up in conversation and that darn tape gets going in the back of my head. Then I am "off to the races" judging everything about them: what they wear, how they act, how they speak and what I think overall is good or bad about them. And do those judgments, bad enough in themselves, stay just with me? If I am honest, no. I give into the temptation to speak and gossip about another and offer all kinds of opinions about their motives. Who am I to judge them? Why do I do to others what I loathe someone doing to me? If I make one simple prayer this Lent Lord, let it be this one: *"Help me this day to be generous in my love and gentle in my judgments."*

Doer of the Word Received: Write this prayer down and tape it to your bathroom mirror at home. Make a copy and put it in your wallet by the credit cards you go to frequently. That way whether in or out of the house, you have a daily reminder against judgement and gossip, two sins deadly in their impact on both the target and the perpetrator! Pray it faithfully when you are getting ready in the morning and on your daily commute or when you arrive at your desk for the day's work. *HINT: Memorize it.*

Notes:

Tuesday of the Second Week of Lent

FEAST OF ST. JOSEPH, HUSBAND OF MARY
2 SM 7:4-5A, 12-14A, 16; ROM 4:13, 16-18, 22; LK 2:41-51A

Unlike the Gospel of Matthew, where Joseph has a more prominent position in the Infancy narrative, in Luke's Gospel his presence is more muted and subdued. Joseph is not even mentioned by name in this passage.

The passage recalls that the parents of Jesus were religious people, faithful Jews, traveling annually to Jerusalem for the festival of Passover. They experience what untold numbers of parents experience - a child who becomes lost. They are united in their aching anxiety at his being lost and shared astonishment at the questions he was posing to the teachers in the Temple where they find him.

Joseph and Mary are inseparable in their faith, in their deep love for this child, in their anxiety, and in astonishment. It is clear they must still grow in their understanding of Jesus' identity and mission. "Did you not know that I must be in my Father's house?"

During this Lenten season, may we grow in our love of Christ, deepen our understanding of his identity and mission in our hearts and in our world, especially through prayer, works of charity, and a more attentive listening to the Word of God so our Lenten practices may deepen our faith, increase our astonishment, and lessen our anxieties. As St. Thomas Aquinas once remarked: "Some Saints are privileged to extend to us their patronage with particular efficacy in certain needs, but not in others; but our holy patron St. Joseph has the power to assist us in all cases, in every necessity, in every undertaking."

Through our celebration of this feast honoring St. Joseph, we are encouraged to reach out to him in prayer, knowing he is a powerful intercessor for us before God. As the great Redemptorist bishop, St. Alphonsus Liguori reminds us, "But everyone must know that, after the Mother of God, St. Joseph is, of all the saints, the one dearest to God."

Fr. Jay Harrington, O.P.
Professed: 1982
Associate Academic Dean & Professor of Biblical Studies
Aquinas Institute of Theology
St. Louis, MO

Tender Father:
We still need to grow so much in our understanding of Jesus's identity and mission! As you did with Mary and Joseph, comfort us in our aching anxiety when we struggle to understand what is happening around us with family members. When we are astonished by unexpected trials, hurts and slights, give us their courage to ponder these things in our hearts, to deepen our faith in your unseen work and to persevere in an attentive listening to your word. Instill confident reassurance that your will comes on your timetable, not ours. Let St. Joseph, the saint dearest to your heart after Mary, be our comforting, encouraging companion this Lent.

Doer of the Word Received: Take 7 to 10 minutes to meditate before an image of St. Joseph today. Pull several up online and pick the one that most touches your heart. As a person of faith, spouse and/or parent, what does his example speak to you? What does it inspire in your own attempt to live one or all his roles out with fidelity and devotion in your own life? *HINT: Examine the consistency of your daily witness as a person of faith, specifically as a supportive spouse or a loving, concerned parent (or any combination of those three) and resolve to take a concrete step that will enhance your commitment.*

Notes:

Wednesday of the Second Week of Lent

JER 18:18-20; MT 20:17-28

The word 'ambition' has both a positive ("... now that's a young person with lots of ambition."), and a negative ("It worries me that his whole life is motivated by ambition.") meaning. The mother of James and John asked Jesus if her two sons could have the highest places of honor in the kingdom. It was a good request of a proud mother, but it was too ambitious, and the other friends of Jesus were indignant, and perhaps a little envious.

The response of Jesus is twofold. Requesting such an honor would be very costly. The majority of their life would be one of suffering and it would not bring them honor, but it might well bring them the ongoing opportunity to be loving and compassionate. People would remember them, not for their power, but for their ability to love without reservation. In addition, Jesus turns the expectations of most of us to honor power and authority in a radically new direction. "Whoever wishes to be great among you shall be your servant; whoever wishes to be first among you shall be your slave. The Son of Man did not come to be served, but to serve ..."

Who in the society do we consider to be great, famous, or successful? Do they serve us, or do they expect us to serve them? And what are your personal ambitions and expectations?

Fr. Michael Champlin, O.P.
Professed: 1960
Center Director
Thomas More Center for Preaching and Prayer
Webster, WI

Teacher:
Teach me the difference between holy ambition and superficial ambition. Help me confront within myself that same tendency of John and James toward superficial desires for status, prestige and "a place at the table" to demonstrate my importance to everyone. Protect me from the need to shine the light on myself. Rid me of the impulse to be jealous when others have the light shining on them. Rather, let me work hard to focus the spotlight on others, their goodness and their needs. Most of all, help me point to you and your kingdom. Let me be wholly concentrated and focused on being faithful rather than famous or successful. For all fame, success and prestige is fleeting. The only ambition to fame I want is to be known as, "one who knows you." For the gospel tells us to know you is to have eternal life. When I have you, Lord, I have enough...more than enough. I have everything!

Doer of the Word Received: Take 10 minutes at lunch today to stop and examine your ambitions. Are you hurrying up the ladder of success, but the ladder is leaning on the wrong wall of ambition? *HINT: Look at your goals, those stated and those you keep to yourself. They will reveal your true ambitions.*

Notes:

Thursday of the Second Week of Lent

JER 17:5-10; LK 16:19-31

Our reflection during Lent often focuses on ourselves. Our Lenten practices and prayers often serve to improve our own personal spiritual life. This makes sense, as we all begin Lent by having ashes placed on our foreheads while hearing the words, "Repent, and believe in the gospel" or "Remember that you are dust, and to dust you shall return." On the very first day of Lent we are presented with our sinfulness and need for conversion.

There is, however, another focus that is important for us to consider: that is, the relationships we have with each other. The story of the rich man and Lazarus is a profound reminder of the consequences of treating our neighbors poorly. During his lifetime, the rich man ignored Lazarus and was not even concerned with his basic need for food. Lazarus "would gladly have eaten his fill of the scraps that fell from the rich man's table."

Both men die, and Lazarus lives eternally at the bosom of Abraham while the rich man suffers eternal torment. The chasm built by the rich man's treatment of Lazarus is magnified in eternity.

Jesus tells us that love of God and love of neighbor cannot be separated. They are basically the same thing. We begin Lent reminded of our own sinfulness and need for conversion. Believing in the gospel requires us to be concerned about those who are most in need.

Fr. Dennis Woerter, O.P.
Professed: 1991
Campus Minister
Fenwick High School
Oak Park, IL

Gentle Spirit:

How often do I need to be reminded: It's not about me! Even when it comes to good and holy pursuits such as working on my spiritual life, I can become self-absorbed. I may not identity with the gross neglect and selfishness of the rich man's treatment of Lazarus in todays' gospel. But I can be guilty of missing the needs of my neighbor because I don't really see her even though she is right there in front of me. All-seeing Spirit, help me see my beloved Christ in all those around me today. Help me not to miss His many faces in all those I glibly pass by. Help me not to lose an opportunity to love and serve my God in all your varied disguises.

Doer of the Word Received: Take a risk and say, "Hello" to at least three of the people you pass by today and give them an accepting smile. Then offer a brief prayer for the joyful, worried or suffering Christ you just encountered. *HINT: Every human being is another variation of a priceless portrait of Christ.*

Notes:

Friday of the Second Week of Lent

GN 37:3-4, 12-13A, 17B-28A; MT 21:33-43, 45-46

Today we are presented with two stories of sin. In the first, the sin is envy: Joseph's brothers cannot abide their Father's preference for Joseph. In the second story, the sin is greed: the tenants are ready to kill to have the land for themselves.

From what darkness in the human heart do such sins arise? Why do people envy others? Why do people grasp for that which others possess? It begins with the desire to be gods ourselves; with the failure to accept that God is in charge; with the rejection of God's gifts to us as not being good enough. We think God got it wrong and we could do better.

If I realize the blessings God has bestowed on me out of love, I will have no need to envy another's blessings. But if I am blind to those blessings, then I will want what I see in others, thinking I have been shortchanged ... If I am not grateful to God for what I do have in life, then I will feel cheated and want to have what others have.

In a more positive vein, if I love the me that God has made, I will be happy with myself as I am and content with having the necessities of life and not seek the luxuries that others may have.

True love of self and contentment in life can be found only in prayers of thanksgiving and gratitude to God, based on my belief that God loves me and my trust that God will care for me. Without this, I will live in imitation of Joseph's brothers and the land owner's tenants. Let us make Lent not only a time of penance, but also an occasion to take stock of what God has given us and a time for prayers of gratitude.

Fr. Benjamin Russell, O.P.
Professed: 1954
Entered Into Eternal Life: August 11, 2014

Generous Father:

Have I been generous in my gratitude for all you have done and are doing for me? When I am not grateful, the doors of envy and greed, self-pity and resentment start to open. Just a crack at first, but the more I fail to recognize and express appreciation for all you have done for me, the more I begin to dwell upon others' gifts, advantages and blessings, losing sight of my own. Comparisons are always the door to temptation. Guide my gaze back to you. Help me not to be stingy in my generosity. Gratitude is the foundation of a solid spiritual life and a healthy life in general. Most of all, lead me daily to take stock of all you have given me and focus on all that you are to me. This is "the one thing necessary" the gospel teaches.

Doer of the Word Received: Before going to bed, jot down ten things you were most grateful for today. Get started by thinking of the good, everyday things you take for granted (i.e. I got out of bed healthy, someone at work greeted me with a cheerful, "Good morning," Traveling home, someone slowed down to let me go before them). *HINT: If you fill up the list fast, you are prone to be grateful. If ten seems like a lot, well…you have some work to do in the "Gratitude Awareness Department."*

Notes:

Saturday of the Second Week of Lent

MI 7:14-15, 18-20; LK 15:1-3, 11-32

"[God] waits for our tears, that He may pour forth His goodness." These words of St. Ambrose apply as much today as they did nearly 1,700 years ago when he addressed the problem of reconciliation with the Church. How often have we encountered someone who felt their sins too great to be forgiven, their shame to great to live with, their problems too great to overcome? In our own lives, how often have we left relationships in seeming disrepair, resisted something new out of fear, addressed minor issues instead of major ones? As difficult as it is to watch someone else stumble or take ownership of our own struggles, we were created for repentance, revival, and resurrection.

Though many of us might not be brought to tears, may all of us turn our problems, our struggles, our fears, and our pains to God during this Lenten season so that He may, as St. Ambrose said, pour forth His goodness.

Fr. Patrick Hyde, O.P.
Professed: 2010
Parochial Vicar
St. Paul Catholic Center, Indiana University
Bloomington, IN

Savior of Sorrows:

When I am pained and feeling overwhelmed with my struggles, my fears and doubts, I think of you in the garden. You agonized over what had been asked of you. You wondered about your own strength and how to be true to God's will. I think of your utter honesty in telling the Father you feared you were not up to the task; to let this cup of suffering pass from you. But then you summon your courage and walk through your fears to pray: "But your will, not mine." What you candidly don't know how you can do yourself, you inspirationally put in the hands of the Father and trust that if His will asks you to drink of this cup of suffering, He will give you the inner wherewithal to do it. You teach me, Lord, not to depend on my strength, but on that of the Father. Give me the same courage with my own tears of fear and agony, knowing that with a willing heart, my Abba and yours will bring forth only divine goodness.

Doer of the Word Received: Pause in your day and pray the prayer Jesus taught his disciples very slowly. Experience the *Our Father* at greater depth. *HINT: Take at least a full minute so you hear and feel in a whole new way the "Our" in Our Father and savor more powerfully, the mini-prayer within "Thy will be done on earth as it is in heaven."*

Notes:

Third Sunday of Lent

EX 3:1-8A, 13-15; 1 COR 10:1-6, 10-12; LK 13:1-9

An elderly Jewish man once told me, "The essence of the Covenant is that we remember what God has done for us… then act based on that knowledge." Remember, for example, the enslavement in Egypt or the captivity in Babylon— where your human dignity was not always respected—then commit to acting in a manner that will never make another people feel the agony of being debased. Empathize with and care for the poor, neglected and powerless, e.g. widows, orphans, and strangers (anawim). Remember what God did for us, then act in a godly manner toward others. Remember, and then act.

The Gospel enacts this approach to covenant living: "If you knew the gift of God and who is saying to you, 'Give me a drink', you would have asked Him and He would have given you living water."

Every Christian can use this simple approach. I Peter 2:10 asks us to, "Remember once you were "no people," but now you are God's People." Corporately, most nations within the Christian Covenant can recall a time when they were a small, powerless group among the family of nations—and were disrespected, conquered and enslaved. How did God sustain them? Personally, many of our faults can be traced to our failing to remember and failing to act on what we remember. That is the core meaning of this holy Season of Penance: coming to greater self-understanding, then acting in life-giving ways.

Before and during Lent, we Christians take time to remember how God has been and is present to us; we are recipients of choice blessings. A lot of thought is expended on what thing(s) we should "give up" to clarify and deepen our following of Christ. We celebrate with Catechumen their spiritual progress. Perhaps we mature Christians could spend the remainder of this holy Season honing our skills in remembering how God has been active in our lives, and then manifest our thankfulness in service of others.

Jesus' encounter with the "Woman at the Well" presents the quintessential dynamic of judgment that often occurs between Christians and those not of the faith, even between Christians and other Christians. Too often we Christians lament our life without acting to change it. Echoing Prophet Job (3:17) we say, "I want to fly where the wicked will cease their troubling (and the weary will be at rest)" Too often, we remain in confusion, rooted in lack of action! As we prepare to communally remember the saving act wrought by God in Christ Jesus, may the power of remembering spur us into greater action in sharing the Good News that what was does not always have to be. God is always making a way out of no way… making a People out of "no people."

Fr. Thomas Jackson, O.P.
Professed: 1988
Parochial Vicar
St. Katharine Drexel Parish
Chicago, IL

Generous God:
Forgive my lack of generosity in so easily forgetting you throughout my day and all you have done for me. I say my morning prayers and then I move on with my schedule, God, not remembering to stop and check in with you, just to say "hello" and to share with you all that is going on with me. I forget to share with you my gratitude for all that goes right in my day, but am quick to question where you are when something goes wrong. In not remembering you, I don't remember to be conscious of the needs of my fellow brothers and sisters. Help me to remember and to act in my relationship with you and others.

Doer of the Word Received: We tend to be very aware of our sins of commission, but what about our sins of omission? Examine your conscience for those things or people you have neglected. Remember them with a list and develop a plan to act on them. *HINT: Don't be afraid to humbly and courageously ask others what you may have missed or forgotten about… your friends and family will be honest with you!*

Notes:

Monday of the Third Week of Lent

THE ANNUNCIATION OF THE LORD
IS 7:10-14, 8:10; HEB 10:4-10; LK 1:26-38

The greatness of the Blessed Virgin Mary is the greatness of her faith. When promised to be the bearer of her Lord and God, her response is "Behold, I am the handmaid of the Lord. May it be done to me according to your word." (Luke 1:38) She asks for nothing. In fact, she commits herself to a life of complete trust, simple humility, and, perhaps most importantly of all, unceasing prayer and service of Our Lord.

Though there is a clear connection between Christ's Annunciation, His Nativity, and the Cross, we often lose, in the midst of it all, the beauty and marvel, the patience and perseverance of the Blessed Virgin Mary. From His birth until He began His formal ministry, Mary served, honored, and trusted. She never wavered nor doubted.

Today, we are reminded and frankly challenged to persevere in prayer and good works, to love zealously and wholeheartedly, to believe the promises made to you in your Baptism, amplified in your Confirmation, and renewed in Reconciliation and Eucharist, are being realized in your everyday, simple, persistent following of Christ.

When Christ first came into the world in the womb of the Blessed Virgin, she had to wait. She was, however, never static. Even her preparations for the birth of Jesus were filled with loving service and prayerful devotion. As she walked with Christ from his birth to the Cross, she poured herself more and more into devotion.

The fullness of Christ, the hope in times of sorrow, the absolute joy of His Resurrection fills those who persevere with Mary through trials and, especially, at the foot of the Cross. "Behold, I am the handmaid of the Lord. May it be done to me according to your word."

Fr. Patrick Hyde, O.P.
Professed: 2010
Parochial Vicar
St. Paul Catholic Center
Indiana University
Bloomington, IN

Generous Father:
Your gift of abundance in the choice of Mary to be your beloved Son's mother, and ours as well, is staggering to fathom! In Mary we find the font of all spiritual gifts, an inexhaustible example from which we can continually draw nourishment and sustain our own devotion in the enduring measure of hers. Convict us with her constancy of purpose, her persistence and perseverance in prayer that we may truly make it our own. Even amid our doubts and struggles, especially amid them, may we pour ourselves out again and again. May we avoid complacency and actively wait in unceasing love for Love's appearance in this moment, at this hour, on this day!

Doer of the Word Received: We may not tell big lies, but we can all be guilty at times of the little white lies, exaggerations, and half-truths. Where have you been less than honest recently and with whom? Clean it up and make amends. *HINT: God will put that less than honest situation and the person who needs to hear from you on your heart. Honestly ask and honestly listen for His guidance. Then act!*

Notes:

Tuesday of the Third Week of Lent

DN 3: 25, 34-43; MT 18: 21-35

Peter is great at asking the difficult questions—the questions which we are afraid to hear the answers to. This time, it has to do with the persistence of forgiveness. Often it is more difficult to forgive than it is to apologize. When someone has wronged us and they come to apologize, we are automatically placed in a position of power. The person seeking forgiveness is vulnerable, admitting fault and standing before us hoping for our pardon and reconciliation. It is tempting to hold onto this power—to use it for our own devices or to "get back" at the person who wronged us. Forgiveness, therefore, is an act of humility—a rejection of the power we gain and a commitment to love and reconciliation.

Forgiveness is a two-way road--we are not always quick to receive forgiveness, either. Bogged down by our faults and tempted to despair by the evil one, we run the risk of falling into the misconception that we are not worthy of the forgiveness granted to us. We must look past our human faults and failings and, driven by Love, accept the forgiveness offered us. It is through this reconciliation that we come to know God— the all-loving Father who promises to "forgive us our trespasses, as we forgive those who trespass against us."

Fr. Samuel Hakeem, O.P.
Professed: 2011
Parochial Vicar
Blessed Sacrament Parish
Madison, WI

God of Forgiveness:
You tell us to forgive seventy-seven times seven, an absurd, irrational act of mercy from a logical, human viewpoint. But your thoughts are not our thoughts and your ways are not our ways. Teach us your way of forgiveness. We so often cling to our grudges like precious jewels that we can't live without. They become us. They take us over and begin to define us. We think we relinquish power when we forgive rather than become even more powerful in you. Rather, any time we act as you would act, we become more like you, more divine, more God-like, in presence and impact. Show us especially how to forgive ourselves. Beating up on ourselves for our past sins brings you no honor and glory, but breeds a perverse pride as well as being a big waste of time and energy. What honors you is a humbled heart and a remorseful spirit that, now knowing true forgiveness, acts out of a profound gratitude in giving that same gift to others.

Doer of the Word Received: Forgive someone today whether they are asking for your forgiveness or not. Ask God for His forgiveness. No slight or sin is too small to mention when seen in the light of all-accepting love. *HINT: The person to forgive is the first person that immediately came to mind praying this meditation. You know who they are. Do it! Your God is with you!*

Notes:

Wednesday of the Third Week of Lent

DT 4: 1, 5-9; MT 5:17-19

Why do what's right? In our Church and society, we often talk about what is right, just, moral, etc. without ever discussing why being good matters in the first place. These reasons can be vastly different. Some are driven by the desire to get into heaven while others just don't want to go to hell. Some follow rules thinking they are necessary for a functional society, though the rules themselves don't mean much of anything. Some think the whole point is to be a caring person (so don't worry about rules or laws if they get in the way of caring).

As Moses exhorts the people to follow the commandments, notice the reasons he gives. You should follow the commandments that you may live; to give evidence of your wisdom; that other nations will honor you; because you remember what you have seen God do. Moses doesn't say, "of course we all hate these rules but without them it would be chaos!" Rather, he affirms the commandments as wise and life-giving; following them makes one a light to all the nations. That is easy to see with some precepts - no one claims that permitting murder would make us better - but do we think of gossip and honesty the same way? Do we see giving to the poor as inherently good, a mark of wisdom and goodness, or just something I have to do to appease God?

Of course, it isn't easy to always think this positively. I admit that I often follow traffic laws because I don't want a ticket and not because I am concerned with the safety of society. I end up trying to not get in trouble rather than striving to be like God. In those moments, I find the final reminder from Moses particularly helpful: do not forget the things which your own eyes have seen. The people at the base of Mt. Sinai had seen God's saving power at the Red Sea. They had personally witnessed God's love for them - freeing them from slavery and giving Moses directions for being a free and holy people. They are to teach and follow the commandments because of how much God has loved them. In doing so, they will become like God and a light to all the nations. We also are called to be holy, demonstrating our wisdom through our deeds, not to earn God's love but because God gives it so freely. We may not have seen the Red Sea split, but we have something greater: the passion, death and resurrection of Jesus - the one who fulfilled the law. Do we remember this and allow it to make us like God?

Br. Joseph Trout, O.P.
Professed: 2011
Theology Department Chair, Fenwick High School
Oak Park, IL

God of Wisdom:
Make me wise. Give me wisdom to truly live and not just go through the motions of my spiritual life. Help me remember what I have seen you do; all the times you have led me from the darkness of foolish choices to the light of reason and prudence. All the times you have pulled me out of self-inflicted follies and revealed my subtle but devastating enslavements to self-esteem, pride, lust, power or material possessions. Allow me to easily remember things I have seen when I properly focus my gaze on you and not myself. Then, in that act of remembering, I show evidence of your wisdom in my life; wisdom that becomes a light by which you guide others through me. To strive to be you in all things is what I most want, God.

Doer of the Word Received: Examine the motives for your actions over the last 24 hours. Did you do the right thing out of love or fear? If you did the wrong thing, what "slavery" to selfish desire does it speak to? Identify in the Notes section one questionable motive behind a choice you made and what it revealed about an attachment which still enslaves you at times. *HINT: Look at whether you acted out of your feelings or your values.*

Notes:

Thursday of the Third Week of Lent

JER 7:23-28; LK 11:14-23

Dorothy Day, founder of the Catholic Worker movement, once said: "God does not demand success of us, but fidelity!"

And so, it was that she committed herself to live one of the highest goals imaginable: to be a peace-maker, to bring about an end to war, to replace all violence with compassionate love. Faithfulness to that goal remained the center of her life through her writings, her hospitality houses, her protests and non-violent actions, her civil disobedience and time in jail. Her successes were few; her fidelity was astounding.

Yahweh repeats the message to the Israelites that He wants to be their God and He wants them to be His people. But He tells Jeremiah that they have resisted the prophets' words in the past, and that they continue to harden their hearts, stiffen their necks and turn their backs.

And even with Jesus' ministry of miraculous healing and casting out of demons, some people still rejected his power and authority as being from God.

Yet Jesus continued his task of healing and preaching; Jeremiah kept proclaiming the word God gave him; and Dorothy Day remained faithful to her prophetic mission until the last weeks of her 83 years of life.

The dose of reality that hits us because of our own failures and frailties and frustrations has the potential to move us to even greater fidelity to what we know God has called us.

Fr. James Barnett, O.P.
Professed: 1959
Limited service
Chicago, IL

46

Compassionate God:
To be compassionate means "to suffer with." When you told us that you wanted to be our God and us to be your people, you welcomed us into your work of compassion. You were inviting us into your mission of "suffering with." Why you choose to work though us, we don't know, Lord. You seem to delight in using human beings as instruments of your marvelous and saving deeds. Help us to not be afraid of joining you in this holy effort. It's not all on our shoulders. We are the workers bees. You are the master builder. You don't ask that we be successful, but faithful... faithful to our part of the work and mission of compassion in the corner of the world you have entrusted to us. Like Jeremiah and Jesus, help us to keep our gaze on you and not ourselves. We know you will ultimately complete the good work you have begun in us, the work of "suffering with" another so the grace of your healing compassion can be fully experienced.

Doer of the Word Received: Who is suffering right now in the corner of the world entrusted to me and what am I doing about it? Who needs me "to suffer with them?" Identify that person. Throw your precious schedule out the window and give them your sincere time and attention. *HINT: Who is that person that just popped into your head? That's the one who needs you.*

Notes:

Friday of the Third Week of Lent

HOS 14: 2-10; MK 12: 28-34

"You have collapsed through your guilt." These words of Hosea speak to the land of Israel as they forgot the covenant with God, and ignored the needs of their neighbor. But they also speak to all who are burdened by sin. How many times have you wanted to just collapse and forget the sufferings of life? How often have you carried your burdens on your back, and not sought help? Well, here God answers his people, saying "I will love them freely." God's love does not come with conditions, or a price, it has no qualifications, it does not burden you, but takes away your insecurities and your faults. And that is why the greatest commandment is to love God with your whole heart, with all your understanding, and with all your strength. In other words, love God with your whole being. Jesus then calls us to love others as we love ourselves, because we are lovable in the eyes of our Father. And if God loves us, even though he has seen the depths of our guilt, then why can't we as well?

Fr. Jude McPeak, O.P.
Professed: 2008
Promoter of Vocations
Chicago, IL

Loving Father:

As the psalmist says, "Our sin stares us in the face." When we are utterly honest with ourselves, we can see our sinfulness and short-comings clearly. Hosea captures the temptation that often arises: to "collapse in our guilt." When we do, extend your arms so that you catch us. Let us collapse in your embrace and soak up your forgiveness and healing reassurance all is not lost. Help us to savor your forgiveness, to know from the feel of your bountiful arms encircling us, that we are still loveable, still the apple of your eyes, still the ones you are referring to when you declare: "I will love them freely." We may be a mess, Lord, but we are your mess!

Doer of the Word Received: Take 5 to 10 minutes today and rest your head on the Lord's chest like the beloved disciple John. Resting near Jesus' heart, talk candidly and trustingly with your mutual Father about the things you regret, are not proud of, and the things you are still struggling with. At the end of your time, feel the Father's arms wrap around you. Don't leave without feeling the acceptance of His divine embrace. *HINT: Find a private place where you will not be disturbed or distracted. Don't just turn your cell phone off. Leave it in another room!*

Note:

Saturday of the Third Week of Lent

HOS 6: 1-6, LK 18: 9-14

When I was in 2nd grade I remember Sister Frances Patricia telling us that God would never send us more than we could handle. He also sent us grace with which we could bear each challenge. In this reading, Hosea seems to be of the same mind, saying: "In their affliction, they shall look for me; 'Come, let us return to the Lord, for it is he who has rent, but he will heal us; he has struck us, but he will bind our wounds'." Hosea one of our prophets, begins with his own struggles with his wife's unfaithfulness and the pain it caused him (which symbolized faithless Israel). Through each challenge he remains faithful and could not give up his wife even when she played the harlot. Hosea was emotional and quick to anger but also knew the saving grace of forgiveness. He talked about the relationship between God and Israel in terms of marriage and Israel's unfaithfulness. In each of our lives there are relationships which challenge us. This lesson from Hosea assures us that challenges will come but with them God sends his grace, strengthening us for the challenge. We grow in our faith, hope and compassion like Hosea knowing the saving grace of forgiveness.

Br. Benedict Baer, O.P.
Professed: 1966
Entered Into Eternal Life: August 26, 2012

Gentle Spirit:

Be gentle with us as we make our way through life's daily challenges. Help us bear them with grace and courage that we might know the secret Hosea knew: We are never without God's grace in times of trial or temptation. We do feel alone at times, abandoned and alienated from you, Holy Spirit, so help us remember you never leave our side. We leave yours. Too often we go looking for consolation, advice and solace in other places, many times the wrong places. We forget we only need to stop and look within, and you are there; to guide us, reassure us, to build us anew when we have fallen. You will show us the way and renew our spirits. You will show us the saving grace of constant forgiveness. Help that truth to register not just in our heads, but in our hearts; not just in the good times, but the bad, not just when all is light, but when the darkness of life threatens to overwhelm us.

Doer of the Word Received: It's the weekend. Take 20 to 30 minutes for some solid, nourishing spiritual reading to build trust in God's constant presence. *Hint: Pick that book that you have really wanted to get into, but told yourself you didn't have the time. Now's the time!*

Notes:

Fourth Sunday of Lent

JOS 5:9A, 10-12; 2 COR 5:17-21; LK 15:1-3, 11-32

Some years ago, *#firstworldproblems* was a trending hashtag. Videos, both serious and sarcastic, told of people from wealthy nations complaining about a lack of free WiFi, or a mobile device running out of power, or even an incorrect coffee order. When a majority of the human population lives without access to safe water and a toilet, these seem trivial. I sympathize with the older brother from the parable of the Prodigal Son. His complaint is ultimately like that of people getting frustrated by *#firstworldproblems*. It signifies a lack of perspective and appreciation.

Through the Incarnation, Passion, Death, and Resurrection of Jesus Christ, we have been reconciled to God, offered friendship with God, and even allowed to Hope in eternal life where we will be permitted to share in God's Divine Life! Like the older brother in the parable, we have already been given everything. And unlike the older brother, who might legitimately complain that his brother's return might threaten his share of the inheritance, the Kingdom of God is like the light of a candle…it is not diminished when it lights another candle. Rather, the fire that provides the candle's light is increased by its sharing. The amount of light increases.

This is how St. Paul in his letter to the Corinthians can boldly state that every Christian is an ambassador for Christ with a ministry of reconciliation. Because we have been reconciled to God and become the adopted sons and daughters of God, our candle has been lit by God's grace and now adds to the light of the Kingdom of God. If God can use us to light another candle, the Kingdom of God can shine even brighter in a world darkened by sin. Perhaps that illumination might help more of the prodigal sons and daughters of the world find their way back to the Father!

Fr. Patrick Tobin, O.P.
Professed: 2004
Spiritual Director, Dominican Shrine of St. Jude
Chicago, IL

Christ Jesus:

I want to be your ambassador, especially in those places that are most scary to go. I need your fortitude to go into the daily landscape of my life and be willing to speak your word of truth and love to a world not always interested, downright indifferent or often openly hostile. Lord, show me how the communities of my everyday life are missionary territory to bring your perspective and worldview to life's challenges. You are the fire that lends the light to my candle. Give me the strength now to share those glowing embers of my light with other potential candles just waiting to be lit by the graced fire of your reconciling presence.

Doer of the Word Received: Ask Our Lord today for insight into where you can be a bridge to reconciliation. What specific family, friend or work situation needs an "Ambassador of Christ" to affect a healing reconciliation? Ask and then listen for the answer, throughout the day, even until the next day. When the Lord lays the answer upon your heart, act on it in his name. *HINT: God usually points us to an answer right in front of our face and under our nose!*

Notes:

Monday of the Fourth Week of Lent

IS 65:17-21; JN 4:43-54

It is not uncommon to hear stories of desperate parents going to great lengths to obtain medical attention for their sick child. In a survey done a few years ago eighty percent of the respondents indicated that they would give their life to save their child. Only sixty percent said they would give their life for their spouse. This gives us insight into how important children are to their parents. In today's gospel we encounter a father who is urgently concerned for his boy who is seriously ill. His motivation for seeking out Jesus is not faith but simply parental concern. There is no indication that he is at all interested in who Jesus is. He is willing to endure an insult to get what he wants even though in another context he would have punished Jesus for such disrespect.

His endurance is rewarded, but he gets more than he sought. He is given the gift of faith.

How often our prayers of petition are shaped by a particular need, but these prayers lead us to a deeper faith. We learn in desperate times how much we need Jesus. Even when it seems our prayers are not answered the way we want, we come to believe in a new way. The key to this story for us is to understand humility in our prayer. No matter our social status, education, or wealth, we stand before God as humans, always dependent, always in need. It is in this context that we come to believe.

Br. Ed van Merrienboer, O.P.
Professed: 1963
Director of Faith Formation
Blessed Sacrament Parish
Madison, WI

Faithful God:

How often, I wonder, even doubt, whether you hear my prayers. As if even one of my mere glances toward heaven can escape your attention! Yet, many times I worry I am just talking to myself when I am praying, or my prayers are getting lost out there in a great abyss of nothingness. Foolish of me, I know. How often have you assured me that if I knock, the door opens, If I seek, I will find? You hear every one of my prayers of petition. They knock at the door of your heart and you open your heart wide to them. It's just sometimes you say, "No," or "No, not yet." Your perspective is larger than mine, your timetable more trustworthy. Give me a deeper faith to keep coming and humbly asking for all I need, for in your will is my peace. Help me to have the faith to really live that fundamental truth out in my daily life.

Doer of the Word Received: Stop by your parish church, your Catholic campus center, or a hospital chapel on the way to or from school or work today. Exercise a humble dependence on God by going and asking for what you need. *HINT: Don't simply ask for yourself. Ask on behalf of someone else that their need, pain, or fear might find relief.*

Notes:

Tuesday of the Fourth Week of Lent

EZ 47: 1-9, 12, JN 5: 1-16

Actions speak louder than words. We do not know of anything that Joseph said, but we know how he responded to threats to his faith and family life. His thoughts were troubling, and then he heard God's communication in his dreams.

Life giving waters flow from the Temple, the sign and place of God's presence for the Israelites. The flowing water gives life, abundant life and even transforms the dead sea's waters into abundance of life with fish and plants giving food and medicines to the people.

The movements, bubbling up of the waters in the pool called Bethesda are seen as healing waters for the infirm. Jesus sees one man lying on his mat ill for thirty-eight years, a lifetime. Jesus takes the initiative and says: "Do you want to be well?" Were I the man, I would shout YES!! WILL YOU!! But the man needs help, is alone, not only ill, but without friends or caring people to help. Jesus speaks his word of healing, "Rise, take up your mat and walk."

Jesus' word is the source of healing. The man doesn't fully understand the sign: the word and person of Jesus are the source of life and healing. Jesus is the new temple, the new sign and source of giving life and healing every day, and on the Sabbath, as the Father gives life every day in the creation of new life and calls us from death into eternal life.

Does Jesus ask us what we need today? What do we long for, hope for? Do we need encouragement, courage to risk instead of holding back in fear? Do we need to understand? Or do we need to be the helping hands reaching out to those who are stuck when they want to move to new life in Christ? Can we see those in need as Jesus sees and act without concern for the naysayer?

Fr. Paul Johnson, O.P.
Professed: 1953
Limited service
Chicago, IL

Physician of the Soul:

Too often we think we can be our own physician, diagnosing and medicating ourselves with homemade remedies. We think we know better than you what we need and how and where to find it. Give us the foresight this Lent to turn back to you as the true physician of our soul and allow you to heal all that is broken, battered, bruised and buried within us. Your words and presence among us is what heals us. Let us open our hearts to you today and take down the "No Vacancy" and "No Trespassing" signs posted to keep you and others out. In the temple of my soul, let me make room for your life-giving waters to flow again, unimpeded by fears or doubts. Let confident hope in your healing reign instead. For the question you address to the man at the pool called Bethesda: "Do you want to be well?" is the question you address to me every day. If only for today Lord, hear my emphatic, "Yes!"

Doer of the Word Received: Admit to someone you trust where you most need healing, emotional, spiritual or psychological. In speaking the truth out loud, pray for the courage to allow the barriers to healing to be brought down. _HINT: What topic, issue or person do you always instinctively avoid talking about?_

Notes:

Wednesday of the Fourth Week of Lent

IS 49: 8-15; JN 5:17-30

How quickly four weeks of Lent pass by. We have heard many encouraging words of God through the Prophet Isaiah. Last Sunday, Laetare Sunday, we were told to rejoice! The Scriptures constantly encourage us to know and believe that God is Love; the Lord is kind and merciful. God knows the difficult paths we have to take in life. Today's readings remind us that God wants to make things easier for us. God has a mother's instinct and will never forget us. Jesus says he and his Father are always working for our good and our salvation. Jesus wants us to follow the way of Love; the way of mercy, forgiveness and compassion.

Let these days of Lent remind us to seek the help of others, and to help those amongst us who need our help-all in the name of Jesus! The journey during Lent should lead to the death of sin and selfishness in each of us, but also to new life and joy, a share in the resurrection of Jesus!

Fr. Gilbert Thesing, O.P.
Professed: 1960
Pastoral Assistant
St. Dominic Parish
Lagos, Nigeria

Loving Father,

The psalmist says you are "slow to anger and abounding in love and kindness." How many times can you remind us of this absolute truth about yourself, that you are a God of unconditional, everlasting love? If the journey through Lent has taught us anything so far, it is the depth of your kindness and mercy, your protection on our behalf always and everywhere. Today, help me reflect that consistent and faithful love to all I meet. Help me to mirror your mercy in the smallest of gestures. Help me to be slow to anger and abounding in love and kindness to all I meet. In the name of your beloved Son, Jesus, let me share the joy of new trust that comes out of a contrite heart and repentant spirit, for your mercy is constant for the one who seeks it constantly.

Doer of the Word Received: Amid your day's comings and goings, hustle and bustle, mentally pray the Divine Mercy Prayer that builds up our confidence in God's fidelity to us: "Jesus, I trust in you." *HINT: Write it down on a slip of paper and carry it with you so that every time you put your hand in your pocket, you are reminded to pray.*

Notes:

Thursday of the Fourth Week of Lent

EX 32: 7-14, JN 5: 31-47

Today's reading from Exodus makes it seem as though Moses were saving Israel from God. "Let me alone," God says to Moses, "that my wrath may blaze up ... to consume them." It is Moses who pleads, "Why, O Lord, should your wrath blaze up against your own people?" Psalm 106 reinforces this interpretation, "Moses, his chosen one, withstood him in the breach to turn back his destructive wrath."

So, when Jesus says that even Moses will accuse those who do not accept him he is asserting that those who refuse his message are even worse than the idolaters of Moses' time. This is surely John's meaning. For him Jesus is the Son whom the Father sent into the world for its salvation. To reject him is to cut yourself off from the new Moses given to intercede for us.

The purpose of Lent is to reinforce in our minds the all-embracing role of Jesus in God's plan for our salvation. By fasting, we are to assert that Jesus is our Bread of Life and to recall that earthly consumption must not distract us from the true source of the life given us from above. By our works of charity, we are to recognize Jesus' presence in the starving millions who share God's world with us and who are in desperate need of our generosity. By prayer, we are to embrace our Jesus whom the Father gives us as a brother to support us. It is Jesus who is to plead for us as we struggle to overcome the sinfulness we inherit from Adam and Eve. Jesus, intercede before the Father for us all.

Fr. James Motl, O.P.
Professed: 1956
Entered Into Eternal Life: April 22, 2016

Spirit of God:

In Lent, we are challenged to go without to remember to go within... where you dwell, shaping and molding us into an *Alter Christus*, another Christ. There we find "the new Moses" who promised to plead before the Father for all time on our behalf. In this way, Jesus continues to be our salvation. Help us never, in even the smallest way, let ourselves be cut off from Him, for then we cut ourselves off from our Savior. Remind us through our fasting this Lent of the real bread for which we hunger, our Lord Jesus Christ. Remind us through our works of charity and almsgiving we must be bread for others who hunger in imitation of Jesus. Remind us through our prayer who is the true source of life-giving nourishment. Remind us, Spirit of God, again and again, for all our problems begin in our failure to remember and our propensity to forget.

Doer of the Word Received: Today, fast from a food or drink you routinely buy. Use that money to buy something for a needy person, purchasing a sandwich or drink for them. Say a prayer for the person you are drawn to help. *HINT: The person is someone you are already familiar with, perhaps even pass by every day. Ask their name and tell them yours.*

Notes:

Friday of the Fourth Week of Lent

WIS 2:1A, 12-22; JN 7:1-2, 10, 25-30

At the Holy Eucharist we hear in John 7:28-29 that "So Jesus cried out in the temple as he was teaching and said, 'You know me and also know where I am from. Yet I did not come on my own, but that the one who sent me, whom you do not know, is true. I know him, because I am from him and he sent me." These words Jesus spoke in the temple as the temple priests were seeking to arrest him for the crime of blasphemy. The son of God, however, did not become man to replace God the Father whose "firstness" or principality are irreplaceable, but to speak in His Name, although the Eastern Orthodox Churches mistakenly accuse the Catholic Church of failing to teach this. Thus, when we listen to Jesus in the Gospel, we hear the very truth of God and that is what we should be reflecting on in Lent.

What is God telling us through Jesus and his Catholic Church? It is that He created us in grace, but our ancestors misused the free will He had given them and rejected His way for them, choosing instead their own way that leads to the loneliness of Hell. God out of love, however, sent his Son as the Jewish man Jesus, conceived by the Virgin Mary, to show us again the true way to union with God by the greatest possible sign of His love, Jesus' voluntary death on the Cross. Therefore, in Lent we practice prayer, charity, and fasting to become more like Him. "So Jesus cried out in the temple as he was teaching and said, 'You know me and also know where I am from. Yet I did not come on my own, but that the one who sent me, whom you do not know, is true. I know him, because I am from him and he sent me."

Fr. Benedict Ashley, O.P.
Professed: 1942
Entered Into Eternal Life: February 23, 2013

Beloved Son of God:

We do know you and where you come from and the One who sent you, our heavenly Father. Your great gift to us reveals the invisible Father through your visible presence. You do not come of your own accord, but because the Father sent you to us that we might know of His love and plan of salvation for us. Grateful for this profound gift, help us Lord, to become more fully who we are: beloved sons and daughters as well, sent out on mission. May we be true to our calling to be sent out to reveal the Father's loving plan: to gather all together as one family. Rouse us from simply being sleepy spectators who hear the Word you speak to us. Lead us to become courageous "doers of the Word" received. May we then please and delight the Father with our obedience to being sent as you did in your unwavering obedience.

Doer of the Word Received: Before the day ends, talk to someone about your faith to foster their own. Act like the beloved son or daughter you are and be obedient to how and who God sends you to. *HINT: It may be someone under your own roof.*

Notes:

Saturday of the Fourth Week of Lent

JER 11: 18-20; JN 7:40-53

"May the working of your Mercy Lord direct our hearts," so this liturgy prays today. There's a Lenten hymn that sings how compassion "walks the city streets and listens for uncertain feet- that seek a home they cannot find." These words make me, an old man, wish I were again a youth-able to again walk the streets of my neighborhood, here at St. Pius. Our Brother David Stazak, O.P., did just that. "Compassion," the hymn goes on, "walks where life is hard, where eyes are blank, and focus marred with pain too great to understand."

Fr. Vincent Blake, O.P.
Professed: 1945
Resurrection Life Center
Chicago, IL

Merciful Lord:

So many things, people, tasks and texts clamor for my heart's attention! Direct my attention back to you where all people and things need to be centered, especially me! Centered in you, I begin to see my neighbor as you see them. Looking through your eyes, I harness reservoirs of compassion and mercy I did not know I had. Help me empty them all this Lent, spending every last drop, especially on those I walk by, but fail to see; those I hear, but to whom I fail to listen to; those I look at, but fail to see. Take me out of my comfortable cocoon and show me your face in all its varied disguises today that I might share the fragrance of your divine presence with all whom I encounter.

Doer of the Word Received: Actively practice seeing your events, efforts and encounters today through God's eyes, taking on His perspective. How do they look different? Take time (it's a Saturday, after all!) to jot down how this exercise affected what you saw and how you felt about the things, tasks, and people that came your way. *HINT: Title your refection: "A Day in my Life Through Your Eyes, God." Only stop writing when you have nothing more to say.*

Notes:

Fifth Sunday of Lent

IS 43:16-21; PHIL 3:8-14; JN 8:1-11

During the summer months, it is a common occurrence for art exhibits, craft shows, music festivals, and street fairs to be celebrated. More often than not, artisans of all ages and backgrounds are open and welcoming as they bring to life new creations right on the spot. Many times, their artistic skills and talents encourages observers to respond in humble wonderment.

In the story of the woman caught in adultery, the temple area becomes a street fair with Jesus as the sole artisan. His bending down and writing on the ground, not once but twice, draws our attention as it does the attention of the scribes, Pharisees, and presumably all the people who have gathered to watch Him.

What is Jesus drawing in the dirt? We can't say for sure because the story doesn't say.

One thing we do know is that Jesus was not dawdling. Jesus is never ho-humming around stalling for time in other gospel stories. Could it be that Jesus was creatively reminding the scribes and Pharisees that God's promises of land and numerous progeny was the foundation for their faith and not the Law of Moses being used to test him? Did a re-creation of what God's love had done in the dirt encourage the scribes and Pharisees to respond in humble wonderment? For the woman standing before him, did it paint a future of new possibilities described by the Prophet Isaiah: "Remember not the events of the past, the things of long ago consider not; see, I am doing something new!"

Fr. Bob Kelly, O.P.
Professed: 1993
St. Dominic Priory
Demver, CO

God of the Present:
Its so easy for me to get struck in the past with its mistakes, regrets and failed projects. Its so easy for me to focus too much on the future, anxiously preoccupied with its unknowns, fearful of challenges yet to materialize except in my own runaway imagination. You are not a God of the past or of the future, but a God of the present. I miss the "something new" that you are doing in the present, in and through and for me, when I live in past disappointments or nervously ruminate about a future yet to be born. In this present moment of my life, open my mind and heart to the new possibilities you create. Guide me to embrace my part in co-creating something new in the corner of the world you have presently entrusted to me.

Doer of the Word Received: When we wander aimlessly and mindlessly between past disappointments and future worries, we miss the endless possibilities God puts before us in the present. Set aside 15 minutes today to conscientiously examine where, how and in what circumstances you are most prone to living in the past or the future. Who or what in your life suffers the most when you don't dwell in the present? *HINT: What person or what important task was most recently forgotten? Who or what got missed because your head was somewhere else? Start there in your reflection on how it happened.*

Notes:

Monday of the Fifth Week of Lent

DN 13:1-9, 15-17, 19-30, 33-62; JN 8:12-20

We've all experienced the pain and disorientation that comes when we discover a person we thought trustworthy has lied to us. Imagine how miserable it would be if this were always the case—if we couldn't trust anyone, not even ourselves. We humans need truth like we need food and water. Even though we may struggle with lies within and without, we long for and work for a world where we can trust and be trusted.

Today's first reading, the dramatic story of Susanna's narrow escape from the deadly lies of those in power, illustrates the unquenchable human longing for the triumph of truth. We want this story to always be the reality—where the innocent are vindicated and the guilty held accountable. Yet, we know many people's stories don't end like Susanna's. Too often power and lies prevail and righteous people suffer. In such an unjust world, we may cry out to God like Susanna yet wonder why the truth we long for is so elusive.

God's response is perhaps unexpected. Instead of crashing in and setting things right immediately and by force, God became incarnate and let himself become the victim too. Unlike Susanna, Jesus' trial ended not with vindication and the triumph of truth but with an innocent man being overtaken by wicked people and a corrupt system. This of course is not the end of the story. As Jesus says in today's Gospel reading, He is the light; his testimony unquestionable. As Truth itself, Jesus could not be extinguished by the darkness of falsehood. In Jesus' "hour," the false power of sin is exposed and burned away by His glorious light. May we strive to know and become purified by the Light of Christ.

Fr. James Peter Trares, O.P.
Professed: 2011
Faculty Member & Campus Minister
University of St. Thomas
St. Paul, MN

68

God of Truth:
You reveal to us that Truth is not first a concept, but a person, the person of Jesus Christ. Through your beloved Son, you became Truth Incarnate that we might know once and for all who we are and whose we are. With this freeing knowledge, give us the courage to confront the lies in our own lives and to live in the truth that is YOU. Help us rid ourselves of the false and superficial, all that masquerades as Truth. Let the deceptive power of sin within us be exposed and any darkness burned away in the light of your love. Help us recommit to guarding our hearts from all that is not you and to live lives of integrity, within and without. And when this feels beyond our strength, give us Suzanna's humility to cry to you.

Doer of the Word Received: We may not tell big lies, but we can all be guilty at times of the little white lies, exaggerations, and half-truths. Where have you been less than honest recently and with whom? Clean it up and make amends. *Hint: God will put that less than honest situation and the person who needs to hear from you on your heart. Honestly ask and honestly listen for His guidance. Then act!*

Notes:

Tuesday of the Fifth Week of Lent

NM 21: 4-9, JN 8: 21-30

An unfortunate reality we live with is that much of our religious vocabulary is laden with heavy cultural baggage which often leads to us missing the mark of what Scripture and the faith are trying to transmit. Words like "sin" and "evil" strike a dissonant chord in our heart and we wish to shirk the connotations of rules, regulations, and oppressive chains of obligation. And let's not forget phrases like, "Accept Jesus Christ as your personal Lord and Savior so that you may be saved," which often leads to an immediate shutting of one's ears and heart. How is our society, then, going to hear the words of Jesus in today's Gospel, "For if you do not believe that I AM, you will die to your sins?"

Lent is a time for us to do a bit of spring cleaning, to clear the baggage that keeps us from God and to reclaim and revive the freshness of our faith. Our readings today call us to do just that. In Numbers, the Israelites lost sight and forgot the core of their experience: that God, out of love, led them out of Egypt and made an everlasting covenant with them. God reminds them where true flourishing in life lies and offers an opportunity to return to that center. Jesus in our Gospel is saying the same thing when he says, "For if you do not believe that I am, you will die to your sins." The word sin in Greek literally means to miss the mark (target). To believe that Jesus is the I AM, God, the Son of God, the one sent by God, and in all that he has come to proclaim, we surely then are on a path of real living, flourishing and fulfillment. If not, we miss the mark of life and in the end will find ourselves off target (aka die to our sins). Today, let us preach the core of our faith and remind ourselves (and the whole world) of all the ways we sin, miss the mark, and thus offer the opportunity Christ offers us, to return to the center and LIVE lives of flourishing and fulfillment.

Fr. Luke Barder, O.P.
Professed: 2008
Graduate student
Cairo, Egypt

Dearest Jesus:

If I am honest with myself, sometimes I feel I am merely surviving my life rather than living it. Yet, you want me to not only live, but to flourish! What is the baggage weighing me down this Lent? What do I need to let go of so I can let you into my heart and mind more fully? Is it grudges and resentments against others for real or perceived slights? Am I angry with life or even maybe you, for "the cards life has dealt me?" Is it all the stuff, material and emotional, I've accumulated to feel good about myself or to numb some inner pain? Whatever it is Lord, I am so weary of carrying it on these sagging shoulders. I need your help in dealing with it. I don't want to miss "the mark of life," YOU, and die spiritually under the pressure of all this excess weight. Only say the word, Lord, and my soul will be healed, my life fulfilled, and I will flourish centered in you as my great, I AM.

Doer of the Word Received: Sit before our Lord on the cross and make an honest list of the emotional baggage you are carrying. What feels so heavy when you think about it? What would be a relief to let go of if you knew how? *HINT: Start with what you have been resentful about for a long time and move to the unhealthy ways you have been coping with it.*

Notes:

Wednesday of the Fifth Week of Lent

DN 3:14-20, 91-92, 95; JN 8:31-42

If you remain in my word ... you will know the truth and the Truth will set you free." (John 8. 31-32)

Have you been accused of something for which you were not guilty? And, to make matters worse, you never had recourse to a just defense? This is not easy. Jesus understands our plight as He also was unjustly accused and tried. He who had only done good for people was falsely accused. It was He who called Himself the Truth and only after his death would people be able to say, "Truly He was the Son of God" (Mt. 27:54). The truth had only then come to make Him free.

We often read in recent years of prisoners who were unjustly condemned. Today, DNA samples are getting them released from prison after being freed from the supposed crime and unjust sentencing. "The Truth has made them free."

Something similar has happened to immigrant workers who have been unjustly accused and imprisoned or deported. Often, they have had little or no recourse to legal counsel. It is only later that the real truth comes to the fore and they are freed. "The Truth has made them free" (John 8:32).

We who try to follow Jesus try to live honestly and uprightly. Likewise, we try to fulfill our work obligations putting a true value on the work we do: living and acting in such a way we truly follow Jesus who is "the Way, the Truth and the Life" (John 14: 6).

Fr. Patrick Rearden, O.P.
Professed: 1954
Pastoral and Preaching Ministry for Hispanics
Chicago, IL

72

Lord of Truth and Justice:
You teach me biblical justice is not giving another what they are due, but being in right relationship with you and others. The truth that sets us free is that you died for all and rise in all who believe in you and remain in you. To remain in you, to remain in your word, is to stand up for my brothers and sisters who are unjustly accused, persecuted, pushed to the margins because of their social or material or mental poverty. "Remain in my word" is a concrete summons and mandate! It is our life's task. "Remain in my word" means: don't put me on a shelve, keep me at the center. It begins with accepting your invitation to the family meal on Sunday. Not because you need us there, but because of what you want to give us knowing what we need between Monday and Saturday. "Remain in my word" means: don't leave me out of your choices; after all, I know you better then you know yourself. "Remain in my word" means: don't go it alone; when you can't walk anymore, let me carry you. So, Just Lord, let me live these truths and enthusiastically defend them before others by remaining centered not in my word, but your word.

Doer of the Word Received: Begin spending 5 to 7 minutes with the Word of God each day when you get up or right before you go to bed at night. *HINT: Subscribe to a pamphlet with each day's lectionary readings like* Magnificat *or* My Daily Bread. *You can also wipe off your dusty Bible, begin reading it daily starting with a paragraph from St. Matthew's gospel and moving to a paragraph from St. Paul's letters.*

Notes:

Thursday of the Fifth Week of Lent

GN 17:3-9; JN 8:51-59

In the first reading today, we hear that Abram prostrated himself, and God spoke to him. And the verse before the Gospel tells us that "if today you hear his voice, harden not your heart." How often do we wonder if God is present in my life, listening, hearing and answering my prayers? What is God asking of me? How am I supposed to respond? These questions require that we open our minds and hearts to God. We must prostrate ourselves before the Lord, lay down as it were, recognizing that if we want to hear God, we must open ourselves to the moments where God can cut through the obstacles, the busyness and activity of our daily lives. We must soften our hearts and prepare ourselves for God touching us with his love and guiding us in our daily lives.

Lent offers us the opportunity to cut through the obstacles which stand in the way of hearing God. Prayer, fasting and almsgiving help us to empty ourselves, to prostrate ourselves before God, and listen to his words of life. Lent is that time when we recall the wondrous things God has done for us. It offers us the opportunity to hear his voice urging us to keep his words and commands each and every day.

Fr. Michael Winkels, O.P.
Professed: 1972
Expressive Arts Teacher
Associate Technology Director
Fenwick High School
Oak Park, IL

Loving God:
What voices am I daily listening to? If I am honest, yours is not the primary one. You are one among many. Amid so many voices, yours get tuned out. Most times I don't mean to shut you out. Other times, I'm busted! The psalmist is right. I have deliberately hardened my heart so I don't have to deal with what your voice challenges me to do or be. It's so much easier to keep you at a distance sometimes. Soften my heart, oh God. Open my mind to trust that you can only lead me to my greatest good. Give me the courage to confront what is in the way of me making your voice the central one I hear in my life, amongst the endless business and constant activity. But also hold me accountable for those obstacles that I myself put in the way. If I am to be prepared for the many touches of your love and grace in the upcoming Holy Week, I need to deepen my trust right now; that you know me better than I know myself and only want my good!

Doer of the Word Received: Make a list in the *Notes* section of all the obstacles in the way of hearing God's voice in your life. Put them in two columns. The first should contain those you did not create but are part of life circumstances (but that you are still responsible for) and the second, those you constructed yourself. Be concrete and specific, listing only the major ones. *HINT: The first list is related to your job and family life, i.e. work hours, driving your kids to their extracurricular activities). The second is the ways you have hardened your heart (i.e. not making time for prayer at any point in the day). Be honest!*

Notes:

Friday of the Fifth Week of Lent

JER 20: 10-13; JN 10:31-42

We meet Jesus today in the midst of conflict. He has been in an intense conversation with the people gathered around him at the Feast of the Dedication of the Temple. There has been a great deal of division among the people. They have been calling Him "controlled by a demon" and "out of his mind." Yet they have been unable to account for His majestic bearing and mighty deeds and words. To some, he did not fulfill what they expected the Messiah to be. They saw his mighty deeds. They heard his beautiful words of truth. Yet, he is not what they expected or desired. Some of the people in the crowd decide to give Him a direct question, which he must answer directly, and not in parables. They ask Him "Are you the Messiah?"

After a lengthy exchange of words, finally he does tell them plainly. "The Father and I are One." This is a total blasphemy to their ears! Every morning and evening they prayed the Shema Prayer, "Hear of Israel, that God is One." How could this Jesus be God? How can He be equal with the Father? They wanted to kill Him for saying such a thing as this.

They gathered stones to kill Him. Jesus answered them with more questions about their own actions, and their motives for their murderous thoughts. He questions their motives, their knowledge of Scripture, and even tries to explain His mission from the Father. They will not hear Him. They try to seize Him, but He leaves them and goes back across the Jordan to the place where St. John the Baptist was baptizing people and found many people who would listen to Him and believe in Him.

Do we hear Jesus? Are we open to Him, even when He surprises us? Even when we cannot completely understand what He is saying? Have we taken all the hard teachings of Jesus and made them weak and soft by setting them aside as impossible or irrelevant? Do I spend time daily seeking God's Word in the Scriptures, so I can apply them to my life? Am I truly changing, or just going through the motions? In what area of my life do I need change? When do I take the time to "hear" Jesus?

It is of crucial importance to hear and listen to Jesus. There is a difference between hearing and listening. To hear is to acknowledge the sounds. To listen is to respond to what is being said by changing your life. St. James says, "Be doers of the Word, not just hearers of the Word." (See the letter to St. James chapter 1). This is closely related to the word, REPENT. Repent means to change one's mind and implies a change in the way one lives, as well. It is not enough to know; a person must also do. One can know that diet and exercise are good for one's health and life, but one also must follow a good diet and exercise weekly in one's own life. Knowing is not enough. To gain the benefit of knowledge one must put it into practice.

If we are a people who are called to live a life open to continuous repentance, (some large and some small), then we must have a very precise way of living in the world. We must be people aware of the Will of God (Scripture and Magisterium), seeking to know the Holy Spirit who gives us the grace to grow and change (Repentance) , and who constantly asks the Holy Spirit for what we need by name (Prayer). Then we must surrender to God's will and, in this way, become fully alive; free to be who we really are. Know, Seek, Ask, & Surrender; the path to freedom, joy and to real change in your life.

Fr. Simon Felix Michalski, O.P.
Professed: 2003
Prior - St. Dominic Priory
St. Louis, MO

Dearest Jesus:
You tell me to "Repent" so I might know your true freedom and let go of my false, fabricated freedom. Only in your freedom can I recognize you and the Father are one and, in your mutual unity, discover the secret to my own freedom. Until then, I only know division, fragmentation, and alienation, sometimes subtle, sometimes not so subtle. Only in your freedom can I really hear the revelation of my own. I so often listen, Lord Jesus, but don't hear, because I think I know better or am simply fearful of your challenge. Like even those who seized and tried to run you out of town, at times I try to run you out of my head and heart, afraid of the repentance or change you are asking of me. Jesus, don't give up on me. Remind me gently, but firmly, that the repentance you require is simply a change in the direction in which we are looking for happiness; change back to your direction where true happiness is always and only found!

Doer of the Word Received: Make a list of 3 to 5 things you sense the Lord is asking you to change about your life. Rank them in importance and initiate the first change beginning the following Sunday. Only begin the second behavior after the first one has become a clear new habit. It could be to set aside a specific time to pray each morning; to be more constant in supporting a family member or to be more faithful and consistent in your work ethic at home, the office or the gym for your professional, emotional or physical health. *HINT: It needs to be concrete, practical and measurable and will have a positive impact on your relationship with God and others, even if ostensibly for you.*

Notes:

Saturday of the Fifth Week of Lent

EZ 37:21-28; JN 11:45-46

Only one week until Easter. Tomorrow we will join the disciples in laying palms at the feet of Jesus and following him up to Jerusalem for the Passover. In today's Gospel we hear, "many went up from the country to Jerusalem before Passover to purify themselves." Now while the purification of the Jews involved bathing in order to cleanse the body, our purification is far more demanding. As the prophet Ezekiel proclaims for God, "No longer shall they defile themselves with their idols, their abominations, and all their transgressions. I will deliver them from all their sins of apostasy, and cleanse them so that they may be my people and I may be their God. "We must take note of two significant characteristics of our purification. First, our defilement is of the soul and comes when we place our own desires over-against our God and neighbor through false idols and apostasy. In the Gospel, the Sanhedrin chooses to preserve its financial and political power by condemning to death an innocent man, thus transgressing the law. (Cf. Dt 19:15-19; Jn 18:19 - 19:6) Consider: Do we vote for measures and representatives who maintain the status quo or work to change the plight of innocent victims and of the poor? Have we disregarded any of the teachings of the Church preferring our own will to the demands which a Christian life makes upon us? The second characteristic is that it is God who does the cleansing. Jesus Christ works by the power of the Holy Spirit through his ministers to forgive our sins and cleanse our souls of the stain our sins have left upon them. Confession is a free gift of God and your parish priest (as well as others) is standing by to help. When our Lord comes again at Easter, let us be repentant and cleansed so that we may rejoice to be among his people.

Fr. Raymond Bryce, O.P.
Professed: 2009
Parochial Vicar, St. Pius V Parish
Chicago, IL

Jesus the Healer:

What do I desire? What do I truly want? Are my wants and desires in sync with who I say I am as a Christian? Are they surface whims rather than the deepest desires of my soul? The prophet Ezekiel challenges us to no longer defile ourselves with our false idols, those things we start to worship and allow to take the place of you. We know you teach us again and again to repent and even told a leper one day: "Be clean." To repent and to be made clean is to entirely reconsider how we approach happiness and wholeness. So often we get caught up in cultural advertisements for what will make us happy. We buy the marketing that says we can't be happy without having this product, or having what that person has, or looking like they do. What was pure in us becomes soiled when we follow these superficial messages. Help us, Lord, to recognize the false within us and recommit to the true. Our deepest happiness is rooted in your cleansing, purifying love. Lead us back to you, to our truest desires, the ones that bring inner peace and authentic joy.

Doer of the Word Received: Ask God to help you see what your "false idols" are, what, in the end, are superficial pursuits or desires. *HINT: Consult a relative or friend who is always honest with you, perhaps annoyingly so!*

Notes:

Palm Sunday

IS 50:4-7; PHIL 2:6-11; LK 22:14-23:56

Palm Sunday is an overture of the week to come – a preview of the Pascal Mystery of Christ and ourselves. It captures the drama of Christ in two images: King and Criminal. The week takes Him (and us) to hell and heaven. The Criminal is really innocent. The Peasant Preacher is really a king and this man is also really God. And as our eyes and ears wander through the killing field this week, they must also hear and see what is hidden: mainly, the inner life of Jesus – a life of obedience, patience and calm, and a vision of all-embracing love. St. Augustine said "We made death possible for Him. He made life possible for us."

It is the Christ, both Criminal and King, that we will find this week in our own lives, and unlike the Apostles, we will not flee when we see Jesus crucified because we know the end of the story. He will rise again from all that is dead. And since we know that ending, we know our own. We know Good Friday lasts a day, but Easter lasts forever. Amen? Amen!!

Fr. Bob Staes, O.P.
Professed: 1985
Limited service
Chicago, IL

Suffering Servant, my King and my God:
In the unfolding drama of this week, we find the parallel drama of our own life; the acute moments of suffering, all the required dyings to self, but also the numerous, graced resurrections of relationships, life's ultimate, transcendent meaning, and renewed inner spirit. In Jesus's unfolding story, we discover our own story unfolding. And…. we are less afraid because we know if we walk with Him this week through it all, we will once again rediscover that He is our ALL.

So, my beloved Jesus, I offer myself as your special companion this week. I commit to walking with you patiently, mindfully, and with tender love on each day's journey of your Passion. Take me with you through the sobering joy of that last supper with your dearest friends, the agony in the garden, the horror of your arrest and scourging, the shame of being treated as a common criminal on the journey through town to Golgotha. And the final nightmare…. your crucifixion, forsaken and utterly alone. Let me lie with you in the tomb until that mystical moment when your beloved Heavenly Father shakes the foundation of the world with His greatest achievement: your resurrection (and the promise of mine)!

Doer of the Word Received: Be true to the commitment you just prayed. Be there with Jesus through each step of His journey this Holy Week. No excuses! Is there really anything more important that can't wait??? Make this week a priority and you will see at its end how God has really made you the priority of this week! *HINT: At the very beginning of the week, schedule the liturgies of Triduum on your calendar, virtual or paper, and don't let anyone or anything rob you of their graces!*

Notes:

Monday of Holy Week

IS 42:1-7; JN 12:1-11

Today we pray with the powerful aroma of Mary, who anoints the feet of Jesus. She has sat at his feet and now anoints his feet. She knows exactly who he is and the kind of honor he is due. The smell of perfume amid the foul smell of betrayal, jealousy, and looming violence. A sweet moment of stillness amid a gathering storm. An outpouring of homage amid the onslaught of hatred.

It is with that knowledge, and with that depth of love, that she pours out upon His feet this pound of perfumed oil. She lets down her hair,and she wipes the feet of Jesus with her hair. She does not care what others think. She does not seek their approval. She honors the presence of Christ. The room is filled with the smell of perfumed oil. The room is filled with the aroma of extravagant love. She holds nothing back. Mary cherishes him for one bright, fragrant moment, before the outbursts of hatred and violence washes over him and carries him away.

On this first day of Holy Week are we willing to raise our voice, our actions to penetrate the rooms of our homes and communities? Are we willing to pour our lives out, filled with the power of faith, like perfumed oil that fills a room? Then let us begin today!

Fr. Brendan Curran, O.P.
Professed: 1995
North American Promoter of Social Justice
Organizer, Resurrection Project
Chicago, IL

Cherished Teacher:

How far am I willing to go to show you just how cherished you are to me? Do all my gestures and actions, spoken and unspoken, reveal you are the treasured One of my life? I begin with such good intentions, Lord. I begin with such resolution. Yet, it can end there on the path of well-meaning plans and wishes the minute I feel fearful of others' scrutiny, the second I worry about what others will think of me. My mind is off and racing: "Am I wearing my religion on my sleeve? Do I look "holier than thou?" Will people think I am just trying to get attention? What if I look foolish? All I truly want is to sit at your feet and anoint your feet with the presence of my love, pouring out all I am in this moment before you. I want to enter that "sweet moment of stillness" with the One my heart cherishes, safe and unafraid in the knowledge you accept me as I am.

Doer of the Word Received: With Mary's inspiration, go to the foot of the cross today and in the sweet stillness of the moment, pour out your love to the Lord. Do not hold back. Then, anoint his feet with some public gesture of honor, unconcerned what others may think. *HINT: Pray Grace before your public meal or stop and say hello to a person on the street, an employee pushing a broom in a store or the resident assistant in your dorm or the janitor at your office building. Do this even if you are with or around other people.*

Notes:

Tuesday of Holy Week

IS 49:1-6; JN 13:21-33, 36-38

Jesus trusted the love of Judas and Peter, two of his disciple insiders. Now in Holy Week we see the betrayal by Judas and the denial of Peter. (We need only to watch the evening news to see acts of betrayal and denial. A celebrity betrays the sacred love of marriage and seeks divorce, a CEO denies letting-go a possible competitor for his position.)

Any personal betrayal or denial is heart breaking. Jesus experienced this heart break as part of his passion, as he is misunderstood and rejected. Without any bitterness for rejected love, Jesus freely offers himself on the cross. As we journey through Holy Week let our prayer focus on the love Jesus has for us. His death/ rising event tells us of his unconditional love, personally offered to each one of us.

Fr. Bede Jagoe, O.P.
Professed: 1954
Entered Into Eternal Life: August 5, 2014

Intimate Friend:
You know rejection. You have tasted its bitter pill. You have seen its ugly face. There is no more painful betrayal then that by one's own friends. How could Judas and Peter do that to you? Better yet, how could you forgive them? The more painfully honest question, Lord, is how could I do that to you? How could you forgive me all the times you do? Perhaps not in the public or obvious ways, but in subtle but definite ways, I have betrayed you and denied you when I have not stood up for you and the faith you gave me. When I have not taken care of the poor or hungry neighbor you told me was my brother and sister, when I ignored the stranger in my midst or stood by when someone different was taunted and demeaned. Whatever I did not do for the least of my brothers and sisters, I did not do for you. And yet you forgive me when I come to you embarrassed and ashamed at my thoughtlessness, prejudice, ignorance and infidelity. May I be as generous and unconditionally forgiving of others while carrying my daily cross as you have shown in carrying your own.

Doer of the Word Received: Write a letter of apology to someone you have betrayed, offended, ignored or been thoughtless too. _HINT: If you aren't hesitating or a little fearful, you are probably not writing the right person. Risk it. Your integrity is counting on it!_

Notes:

Wednesday of Holy Week

IS 50:4-9A; MT 26:14-25

Every year, the Gospel for Wednesday of Holy Week offers Christians the opportunity to self-evaluate in light of Judas' betrayal of Jesus. Matthew's account of his selling Jesus out for a mere 30 pieces of silver still sends shivers down the spine.

Yet, the purpose of the daily readings is not so much to look backwards as it is to address the present and ask challenging questions of ourselves regarding current betrayals of Jesus, both individually and communally.

What Judas did led to horrific violence. Loving the Lord as we do, it is easy to point the finger at him and cry, "Shame on you!" However, Judas is not the only one capable of betrayal. Some choices made in today's world lead to comparable horrific violence. The support of violence of any kind, be it verbal, emotional, or physical, including international wars, risks our betrayal of Jesus and the selling-out of the heart of Christianity. Is war not a striking example of the failure to understand Jesus' teachings and stance for peace?

Pointing the finger at Judas may not be the most profitable way to receive today's sacred texts. It may better profit Christians to pray the scriptures as honestly as possible and then take a long look in the mirror, while begging God for the grace to remain faithful to our name.

Very Rev. James Marchionda, O.P.
Professed: 1968
Prior Provincial
Chicago, IL

Forgiving God:

Facing the mirror of my own behavior, where am I most tempted to sell you out? Is it the comments I make around the dorm, the office cooler, the lunch room, or even in the church parking lot? Is it when I participate in gossip about another employee or her family? Is it when I stand there saying nothing when I witness discrimination of a fellow student, coworker, or parishioner? Am I tempted to sell out because my popularity, what people will think of me, is more important than the values of the gospel I say I live by? I bear your name, Christian. What is the impact when I don't wear that name, faithfully and sincerely. Give me courage, especially in this the holiest of weeks, to proudly reclaim the name, Christian. To not preach at people but be a preaching among them. I know God we preach first not with our words, but with the very way we live our lives. You trust me to be a walking, breathing preaching every day with the gospel truths as my badge of honor. Please deepen my sensitivity to how I speak, act and walk among people each day. For I am publicly committed to the name above all names, the name for which heaven and earth bow in praise, adoration and worship, your name. May I not sell you out for the fleeting silver of popularity, prestige or possessions.

Doer of the Word Received: Midway or at the end of the day stop and look into the mirror of your behavior. Thank God for the things you are grateful for today, especially the moments where you talked and acted as befitted being His beloved daughter or beloved son in the world. Continue reviewing the day and ask forgiveness for the moments you are less proud of when you played it safe or hid behind, "It's not my problem or "They are not my concern." Finish by asking God to help you to do better tomorrow when you try again to make the world more Christ-like. *HINT: It's about awareness, not beating up on yourself or mere coasting in our Christian witness.*

Notes:

Holy Thursday

EX 12:1-8, 11-14; 1 COR 11:23-26; JN 13:1-15

Jesus, the teacher, the master, the lord, knows he is about to die. There is so much more to teach his disciples, more than he could possibly convey in one night, more than they could absorb. So, he begins not by speaking, but by acting, washing the feet of his disciples. Peter does not understand, which is not surprising, and Jesus says, "I know you do not understand now, but do as I have done, and eventually you will understand." He needs them to understand something they could only learn by doing ... by serving ... learned when the master serves the servants and power relationships are turned upside down.

Do we, who call ourselves followers of Jesus, follow this? Have we learned this lesson that can only come from being servants?

Further, Jesus washed all of his disciple's feet. Judas was still there. Jesus performed this action just before he confronted Judas, reaching out in love one last time. He served not only his servants, but his enemy who would betray him.

Do we, who call ourselves followers of Jesus, follow this?

Fr. Scott Steinkerchner, O.P.
Professed: 1990
Preacher, Food for the Poor
Minneapolis, MN

Trusted Master:

Many times, I do not understand why it had to be this way. Couldn't God the Father have chosen a different way for you and for me? In the washing of the feet you show me that sometimes we can only understand by doing, by following your example of humble service. Things are not on our timetable, but yours. Our place is to be obedient as you were obedient, even unto death…of our plans, our agenda, our particular dreams. Teach us to die to all that is not you, trusting we will forever live in all that is you. Through the gift of your very body and blood, you give us the courage to embrace whatever our current crosses, whatever seems unanswered of earth's prayers sent heavenward and whatever appears incomprehensible to our struggling faith. The gift of your very self this day as nourishment for our souls and the example of your selfless service, are more than enough for us. Empty us of self in imitation of your self-emptying.

Doer of the Word Received: Prayerfully sit before an image of our Blessed Mother. Reflect upon the beauty of her obedient, "yes," and trust in God's wisdom when she did not understand how it would all work out. Pray for a renewal of your trust in God as you walk with Jesus through His passion, death and resurrection in the Triduum. *HINT: Show up! It's the only way trust is built in a relationship.*

Notes:

Good Friday

IS 52:13-53:12; HEB 4:14-16; 5:7-9; JN 18:1-19:42

Good Friday is the ultimate act of love. It is, of course, a paradox that new life comes from death. Nature helps us to understand this mystery as we see new life blooming from the seeds buried in the darkness of the earth.

We are often reminded that there is no Easter Sunday without Good Friday. Many joys in our lives are preceded by our own personal crosses. Brothers carry the cross of diminished health and emotional pain. Yet, often we see in these men a brokenness transformed into holiness. Rooted in the mystery of suffering they will be justly rewarded.

On this day we cannot help but think and pray for those who suffer so unjustly because of greed and the lust for power. The cross is heavy in Syria and Sudan, among the undocumented who live in fear, for battered women and misguided youth. All of us are the beloved of God. We pray for these men and women and for ourselves as we carry our own crosses.

Fr. Michael Kyte, O.P.
Professed: 1982
Entered Into Eternal Life: March 27, 2014

Suffering Servant:
I truly want to be there with you today at cost to my own peace and comfort. I want to stand by you while you are arrested, led away in chains and interrogated by Pilate. I want to throw my body in front of yours with every scourging blow from the guards, put my hands protectively above you so the cruel crown of twisted thorns digs into me rather than the sacred crown of your head. I want to be brave Veronica stepping out to tenderly sooth your bloodied face with my comforting cloth; willing Simon, not hesitating to shoulder the unimageable burden of your cross; the beloved disciple, not running away from fear of the cross, but keeping vigil at its foot with Mother Mary so you know you are not alone, that I want to be, no, am, your faithful friend, your soulmate. I want to be newly converted Mary Magdalen, looking up at you hanging on that wrenched wood of the cross, wanting you to see the look of total and absolute love you gave me mirrored back to you at your most painful hour. I want to be Nicodemas, reverently carrying you down from the cross, helping your grieving mother hold you in her arms as we take you and lay you in the tomb. Lord, I want to be there, so help me to truly be there…no excuses, no distractions…only the acted-upon attraction of giving back to you what you have always given me…Your full and undivided presence whatever the hour.

Doer of the Word Received: Do what you say you want to do…be there in each of the moments! *HINT: Go to the 3:00 service at your parish church or if that is not possible, meditate on the Stations of the Cross from a pamphlet (i.e. Everyone's Way of the Cross by Clarence Enzler is an excellent for personal recitation) or online source.*

Notes:

Holy Saturday

GN 1:1-2:2; LK 24:1-12

During the Christmas Season, we are accustomed to singing, "O holy night, O night when Christ was born." This night, this Saturday night, this night of vigil, is another holy night, a night when Christ rose from the tomb. An ancient homily for this night spoke of something strange happening this night, something the world had never seen before. This night, this holy night, this night divine.

This night takes us back to the beginning, to the Book of Genesis, when God created the heavens and the earth. This night we celebrate creation again, a new creation. This night recalls the promise God made to Abraham. It recalls an earlier Passover, from Egypt to a promised land. But this night, we celebrate the Passover of Jesus from death to new life. This night is that night for which Christmas prepared us. On that night, that Christmas night, God entered the world. The Word became flesh.

On this night, we discover why God became incarnate. On this night, Christ returns to the Father and takes his flesh, his humanity, and ours along with him, back to the Father. This night we too are re-born.

The reading from Romans teaches us that when we are baptized, we are baptized into Christ. In that baptism we are united to Christ; we die with him; we are raised with him. For Paul, we are already raised from the dead. We live the risen life now. We put our old selves away and live something new. This night we are reminded we have been made anew, re-created, born again. We rise with Christ.

In our Gospel for this night, Luke speaks not about the night of death, about a night in the tomb, but about the first day of the week, a new week, a new beginning, when all is being made new, not about an empty tomb, for death was not able to constrain him. O death, where was your victory? O Christ divine! O holy night!

Fr. Don Goergen, O.P.
Professed: 1971
Senior Fellow & Adjunct Professor
Aquinas Institute of Technology
St. Louis, MO

God of New Life:
You who create all things new, create me anew. Give me a fresh beginning in your Word made flesh, wounded and passioned for my sake and risen from the dead. Give me the courage to begin again. Help me to fight the Father of Lies who whispers in my ear that the dye is cast, and I am burdened forever with this sinful flesh without hope of redemption. Let me know all that feels dead in me can rise again, transformed in your victory of patient and suffering love. Teach me how to live again, to be recreated anew in your image and likeness simply for this day, for these 24 hours and to radiate the joy and peace of that new life for others. Help me live my resurrected life here and now in this life. For it is not tomorrow that I rise with you, but today!

Doer of the Word I have Received: Proclaim your faith publicly today, unabashedly wherever you go. Whether while jogging, pulling up at the gas pump or buying groceries, greet people you encounter with "Happy Easter!" or "Happy Resurrection!" Yes, they may think you are nuts or find it uncomfortable, but you will plant a seed of your joyful faith in the soil of their lives God can then till. Publicly professing anything today is always a risk. Lean into the risk and grow from the challenge! *HINT: Don't put it off. Take the risk of discomfort early when you are feeling most empowered by the day's festive moment!*

Notes:

Easter Sunday

ACTS 10: 34A, 37-43; COL 3:1-4; JN 20:1-9

What we celebrate today is first and foremost the Resurrection of the Lord; but there is a little self-interest here, too, since we also celebrate the hope of our own resurrection. Although the resurrection of the body is our greatest hope, it is also what we know least about. We know that we will be transformed, "in the twinkling of an eye," as St. Paul says, but we also know from Scripture that like Jesus, we will be recognizable to others. I always find St. Thomas Aquinas to be a source of inspiration, so I checked out his great work, the *Summa Theologiae*, to see what he had to say about the resurrection. There was some good news and some bad news.

He says, first of all, that we will be resurrected with the same body; that was not such good news, since my body isn't what it used to be, and it is definitely not improving with age. But then the news got better: he also says that after the resurrection we will have hair, and that we will be youthful (*ST* III, q. 79, 80, 81).

The celebration of Easter is full of promise and mystery. As we moved through the days of the Triduum, we knew that. The liturgies of Holy Thursday, Good Friday and the Vigil were awesome and frightening. That is probably why we tend to trivialize Easter with bunnies and Easter eggs and little candy "Peeps." We can barely get our minds around the possibilities of what resurrected life will be like, so we develop traditions that keep the mystery in control, in ways that we can understand. Someone once said that if we really understood what this was about, we would go into Church wearing crash helmets rather than Easter bonnets.

So today as we celebrate, let us each take a few moments of silence to sit back in wonder. Use those moments of silence to imagine Christ's passing from death to life. And then imagine how our lives would be if we really, really believed in the resurrection of our own bodies.

Fr. Charles Bouchard, O.P.
Professed: 1975
Senior Director, Theology and Ethics
Catholic Health Association
St. Louis, MO

Risen Christ:

We feel the light today! Glorious light, life and love bursting forth from that unimaginable tomb of hope, frightening and exhilarating us all at once. You promised you would make all things new. We have lived off, fed off that hope all Lent, all Holy Week and in these passion days of Triduum. Now our hope has become luminous in your resurrection and in the promise of our own. On the threshold of the 50 days of Easter, keep the gaze of our minds and hearts on you as to a candle enkindled anew within us. Help us do nothing to extinguish its flame, but keep it strong and safe from the winds of our own complacency or neglect. Renew our commitment to radiate that light to others through the joyful exercise of our faith, the evident confidence of our hope, and the credible witness of our self-sacrificing love. Risen Christ, may your light, life and love rise in us, radiating out to others!

Doer of the Word Received: Savor the spiritual joy amid a Lenten journey well-lived and an Easter season newly born. Take what you have learned and grown from in your friendship with the Lord into these next 50 days. You have discovered the joy of Lent: growing in friendship with the Lord as a preparation to receive the miracle of the Risen Christ of Easter! Share that joy by being a part of other Christians sharing an Easter meal, whether your immediate family friends or fellow parishioners. *Hint: Don't put that friendship back on a shelf. It's the PEACE the world cannot give. Continue to grow in your relationship with the Risen Christ by putting it front and center. Let others experience God ALIVE in you.*

Notes: